THE CURAE

THE CURAE

AN ANTHOLOGY

FROM THE INAUGURAL

CURAE PRIZE

WITH AN INTRODUCTION BY

ANNA VAUGHT

RENARD PRESS

RENARD PRESS LTD

124 City Road
London EC1V 2NX
United Kingdom
info@renardpress.com
020 8050 2928

www.renardpress.com

All pieces in this volume first published by Renard Press Ltd in 2023

Cover design by Will Dady

Printed in the United Kingdom by Severn

ISBN: 978-1-80447-059-6

9 8 7 6 5 4 3 2 1

All links accessed 1st November 2023.

Renard Press is proud to be a climate positive publisher, removing more carbon from the air than we emit and planting a small forest. For more information see renardpress.com/eco.

CONTENTS

WELCOME TO THE CURAE

A carer is anyone who looks after a family member, partner or friend who needs help because of their illness, frailty, disability, mental-health problem or addiction and cannot cope without their support (I use the NHS definition). 2022 data from Carers UK found that there were approximately 10.6 million unpaid carers in the UK and the NHS Long Term Plan of January 2019 repeated a commitment to improve how the NHS identifies unpaid carers, and to better address their health.

I have been balancing needs for a long time, and I was also a carer for my parents in my teens. The intensity of the last few years has, repeatedly, nearly felled me in terms of mental and physical health; before this I spent a decade trying to find appropriate support and diagnosis. Seven years ago I began writing, in a moment of rebellion. I gave up expecting to have my ducks lined up and just started a book – and I have not stopped. I cannot pretend balancing the multiple roles has been easy, but I do know that writing has given me hope and focus, and it has led me into abiding friendships and new and lasting work possibilities.

Being a carer can be rewarding and, as I am wont to say, it is predicated on love; but it can also be heartbreaking, not just because of what you see a loved one going through, but because of having to find resources, multi-task, contact various agencies and, not infrequently, see it all fail. The notion that *help is out there* is, for many, barely a starting point. There is nowhere near enough help to go round, and I want to be absolutely frank about this because my heart broke over and over: it is not just the lack of resources, but lack of will, and this is true across multiple agencies. That is an almighty challenge. You may already be tired, but you have to advocate and advocate again with education and health professionals, and it feels desperately isolating. I hear this over and over.

What can I do? I thought. I considered the publishing world I had launched myself into and addressed a core belief of mine, which is that creative work is not froth, it is essential, core to our being. I absolutely believe that. So I decided to set up a literary prize for writer-carers and would-be writer-carers to offer other more of that – to try and give others what was not there for me when I propelled myself into the industry. I thought that the prize could be a focus for those who would simply enjoy doing some writing but had no ambitions in that area, and I also had a notion that it could provide access to industry. At that stage, I had little idea how that could happen, but I launched it anyway, with coverage from the *Bookseller*.

I said to them, 'The last few years have been extraordinarily challenging, so I aim to offer the boost I would have wanted for myself. I know first-hand that if you are a carer you may also be battling for support, diagnoses and funding – it's distressing and debilitating – and I want writers to be heard, seen, included and understood.' Within hours of publication,

I was inundated with offers of help from across industry. From writers, editors, mentors, literary agents and agencies, publishers, our union and course providers. Soon after that, I found the brilliant help of authors Michael Langan, Amy Lord and Elissa Soave, and within days we had an offer of publication.

When submissions began a few came through the door – and then a deluge. That was not all: some people just wrote to say hello or to say thank you, though they did not think they would have the bandwidth this year; nonetheless, that the prize existed cheered them along. That really buoyed us up for the monumental task of, between us, reading hundreds of entries. But it was not only that. Something I had not thought of was that people might write at any length in an accompanying email. And they did. All the entries were read anonymously, so they were separated from their email smartly, and it was down to me to read the emails and to reply if I had time or, sometimes, strength. I learned and was gifted so much about people's lives, and I want to say here that I held it – and hold it – in my heart. There were writers caring for multiple people, for their life-limited children or teens, for partners, friends, a neighbour – and for any number of reasons. There were also emails from people who were past carers, whose work we could not accept this first year, and I read desperately sad stories and heard how any attempt at creativity now was too late – the person they had been had gone. In a way, these were the hardest to read. We also had entrants who wrote to tell us that during the judging period the person for whom they were caring had died – and so my husband and I made a little garden at home, and I planted roses for them if they wanted me to, and the roses are named after the lost one.

You know, we will all be ill, all lost and many, many of us will be carers – if not now, then later. Data shows us that, over the period 2010–20, every year 4.3 million people became unpaid carers, which is 12,000 of us a day. It is isolating, but it also binds us together because of its ubiquity, its commonality.

I feel that the Curae is one of the best things I have ever done, and that it is one of the best things to happen to me, since I am merely the person who thought it up and the rest occurred because of others' insight and generosity. Never othering, just respectful, diligent and humane. The prize attracted a wealth of extraordinary submissions; the inaugural prize was widely praised for its inclusivity and spotlighting of neglected talent; and this anthology celebrates the works that made it on to the shortlist. All those on our shortlist found industry opportunities as a result, and I will be staying in touch with everyone. Kate Blincoe and Helen O Neill, our two overall winners, are working with me for a year, on top of industry mentoring, courses, editing opportunities and agent and publisher meetings. I very much wanted the prize, as I said, to be a way into industry if it could be.

Some lovely things happened as part of it all. On a personal level, it solidified for me what I want to do and be in publishing, which is, above all, to be a champion of access and inclusivity – carers are truly a marginalised group – and it gave me hope and direction for my own life. It is hard for me to put into words how important this all feels. Even better, however, is that those who were honourable mentions, shortlisted or winners, found each other and went to create a writing group. I do not really know what they get up to, because obviously I cannot gatecrash, but I hope it is gently productive, fun and deeply rebellious too!

So I hope you enjoy the work in the anthology. Entrants were told they did not have to write on the caring role, but you can see it implicitly and sometimes explicitly in the winning work. It is varied, exciting and I hope to see much more of everyone in this book. For some writers, it is the first piece of prose they have completed; for the vast majority, this is their first published work.

Finally, I am delighted to say that all profits from the anthology will go to the Carers Trust and Carers UK. You can read about their work here:

https://carers.org/
https://www.carersuk.org/

I hope you thoroughly enjoy the book – and to Kate, Helen, Sheena, Sara, Kerry, Jess, Joyanna, Jan, Feline and Emma, and to our honourable mentions, Elaine, Abi, Phillip and Poppy, I am so very proud of you, and I am excited to see what you do next.

ANNA VAUGHT

THE CURAE

Please be advised that many of the pieces in this volume deal with topics which some readers might find difficult, including mental health, eating disorders, drug and alcohol misuse and suicide.

NON-FICTION

ALP 650

Helen O Neill

Liverpool, 1967

It wasn't that we didn't listen to popular music. I mean, you couldn't avoid it in the Sixties, especially in Liverpool, but our soul music was laid down behind our front door, when the radio was turned off and Dad dictated the playlist from his turntable.

My dad was fourteen when he bought his first record, after he heard his fellow coalminers sing '*Va, pensiero*' in four-part harmony in the echoing, subterranean chamber where they washed the black dust from their bodies. After that, he saved his weekly allowance to buy 78-rpm records, and later 33s and 45s. By the time he married my mother he had a small, eclectic collection, a wind-up gramophone for his 78s and a basic record player for the rest. With these, he set the soundtrack to our early lives, imprinting on us the indelible music which would connect us for ever.

We had opera when other kids had The Beatles. We harmonised with Welsh choirs while washing dishes, hummed the melody from Beethoven's Pastoral Symphony as a lullaby and, for giddy winters' nights by the fire, we had 'The Laughing Policeman' and Stanley Holloway. Dad always joined in, either singing or whistling, and for those giddy ones he did the actions, jumping around and gesticulating until our bellies hurt with laughter and tears streamed down our faces. Singing in the car, the harmonies we wove were reflections of the Deep South – soulful, spiritual songs about the Mississippi, sung by white Liverpudlians living by the Mersey. On my first day at school, the teacher asked us to come up in turn and sing our favourite song. I sang '*La donna è mobile*' from Rigoletto, its beautiful Italian mangled by my broad Scouse accent. I'm fairly sure it stood apart from all the little lambs and 'Penny Lane's that the poor teacher had to endure that day.

For every season there was a sound, for every event a musical bookmark, for every silence a record.

Dad's collection was always his place of rest. His records were neatly stacked on special shelves, each one labelled, indexed and meticulously cross-referenced. In the beginning, the top right-hand corner of each cover held handwritten numbers and letters, a mysterious code which linked it to his brown leather-covered drawer of filing cards. Later on, he bought a Dymo Labeller and the numbers and letters were dialled up and clicked out on to hard sticky tape and affixed over the handwritten ones. Funny thing was, he didn't really need the referencing system. He could approach his shelves with his eyes closed and put his hand directly on to any record he wanted, his muscle memory knowing where he had placed it. It was all about the process, sitting for hours on end listening to Gigli or McCormack or Callas, lost in the blue and red writing on the cards, oblivious to everything around him.

I can still see my father removing a record from its sleeve with eucharistic reverence, balancing the rim on his thumb while his index finger fitted beneath the hole at the centre, and bring it to eye level to blow off any dust. I can hear the ritual stroking of the needle three times to check the volume before lifting the arm across and lowering it into the groove in precisely the right place. I see him close his eyes as the needle travels across the disc and the sound carries into the room, and as the last notes fade away, I see him pause. This moment is never hurried. He lets the echo of the music hang in the air before he breaks the connection. Waiting for the incense to dissipate.

Connemara, 1969

That summer of the Moon Landing was the first time I realised my father wasn't perfect, and I was just six years old then, so I only had a few short years to know him as the man who could do no wrong.

At the time, my grandparents were caretakers of a big house near Clifden, owned by one of the Guinness family. When the owners were not in residence, we visited for long weekends, spilling over from Granny and Grandad's small apartment into the 'Big House'. We liked to pretend we lived there, in this grand house that had guest wings, a kitchen with two sinks, a glass case with a stuffed otter in the hall, which was bigger than our own ground floor, and fireplaces so large we could stand up inside them.

On that Saturday morning in July, while the rest of the family were outside on the front lawn, Dad and I were in a sunny room together. It was effortlessly simple, as the rooms of the wealthy are, with a perfection of shabbiness and a casual placing of glossy books and the latest albums on the shelves. I lay on my belly on the bay window seat, kick-swaying my feet, the green Connemara tweed cushions scratching against my cheek, and my hand draped downwards, slowly swinging in an arc, lifting the dust motes to dance in the sunshine slanting across the shiny, wooden floor.

Dad walked his fingers along the albums, whistling in that way he did, hardly moving his lips, his balding head tipped slightly to read the titles. He selected one called *Harry* and handed me the cover, telling me it was Harry Nilsson's new album. I read the handwritten story about a magic lamp on the back of the cover, which was penned by a six-year-old girl, just like me. The cover was signed in flourishing hand by the owner, one Suzie More-O'Farrell.

Dad placed the vinyl on the turntable and landed the needle into the groove with the precision of the lunar module. He kicked off his shoes and sat beside me on the seat, leaning his back against the angled wooden shutter. I sat mirrored opposite him, the soles of our feet touching. We listened to *Harry*, from the beginning until the last note faded away, until the pause. Through the window we saw Mam beckoning us to come outside into the fresh air, but we waited just a bit longer. We were still swimming in the juices of the album, and we stayed to let it marinate.

Months later, I came across *Harry* in his record collection at home – ALP 650 – and I saw the owner's signature, betraying his wrongdoing.

My heart felt a cold fear for him. I wanted to tell his sin at my first confession, and have it absolved, but it wasn't my sin to tell, even though I carried it.

Nenagh, 1972

I followed the music to find Dad, to say goodnight. He was listening to Caruso singing '*Vesti la giubba*' from *Pagliacci*. The album cover was on the table – there was the clown in his motley garb, arms draped dramatically over the back of a chair, with his dark eye make-up dripping down through the white powder of his face.

'Why is he crying, Dad?' I asked.

He paused for a moment and looked up at me.

'It is his job to act happy, but he is sad.'

The sound of my mother's knitting machine zipping over and back was a thousand miles away in the kitchen.

Ridi del duol che t'avvelena il cor...

Laugh at the pain which is poisoning your heart.

Nenagh, 1973

One evening we were waiting for Dad to come home for dinner. Eventually Mam sighed and put his dinner between two plates balanced above a boiling saucepan to keep warm, and we went ahead without him. I pushed my food around, trying to make it look like I had eaten some. It no longer smelled appetising. You can't really eat food when you're anticipating a scene. My younger sister, whose stomach always carried her worries, began retching the grisly meat into her cup of water while our frayed Mam shouted, 'You'll eat it if you have to sit there all night!'

We heard the key foundering a few times before the front door finally opened. Mam's thunderous face turned to him as he came into the kitchen, his eyes red, his breath smelling of danger and the shiny record shop bag swinging from his hand. I knew from his swagger that Mam would have to stretch a pound of mince seven ways for a few days again. Before she launched we scattered like cockroaches, into the dark places out of sight. My littlest sister had to stay, trapped in her highchair. My older brother Michael and I ran into our bedroom, and we sat silently on the bottom bunk, listening as the yelling got louder and louder, across and back, with thumping and clattering, doors opening and closing, running, slamming.

'There's your bloody dinner...' There was a smash as plates bounced off the tiled floor.

'It was only a few after work!'

'Well for you! And what are you doing buying more records?'

'It's that Perry Como one I've been waiting for.'

'I don't care! I don't care! You think more about those damn records than you do about us!'

'Bloody Hell!'

The back door slammed, and the sweeping brush bounced on to the tiled floor with the impact. Michael and I waited. We knew this hiatus would bring something else. It never ended with just the words.

Dad passed by our window, running towards the garage, his wind-up gramophone in one hand and a bundle of 78s under his other arm. His face was red, his frown full of intent, his teeth bared.

Next came a crash and the splintering sound of metal on metal, blow after blow ringing through the walls. We watched shards of black shellac fly out the garage door and into the vegetable patch, planting His Master's Voice among the cabbages and scallions. Then came the turntable and the undulating inner workings of the gramophone, the guts and offal of a butchered beast being cast aside and exposed to the crows and the prying eyes of our neighbours, peeping through their kitchen windows.

We knew what to do without even speaking. With a simple nod we crept along the hall and ducked to avoid the razor-sharp words still being flung like spears from behind the kitchen door, aimed in the general direction of the garage. The hot press clicked open slightly as we passed, and I saw my younger sister and brother sitting quietly in the darkness on top of the clothes in the ironing basket. I held up my hand to them in a silent STAY and the door clicked closed again. Michael and I slunk into the dining room and stood before the tall shelves holding Dad's collection. There were gaps where there shouldn't have been and an irreverent littering of records on the floor. I reached for the precious ones, and Michael grabbed handfuls of others. We staggered back to the bedroom under the weight of them, slipping them under the mattress of the lower bunk, away from the anger and the axe. We made six trips before the chopping finally stopped and he drove off in the car.

Mam pretended that everything was all right, carrying on as if nothing had happened. We were expected to do the same.

I slept on the floor that night in case I crushed the records. I pulled my blanket over my head to stop hearing Mam crying on the phone to Granny, telling her what a bad man my daddy was.

Dublin, 1985

That August I was getting married. For sure, it was for love, but it was also a means to an end, a chance to escape. The bouquets of flowers and Waterford crystal wedding gifts on display barely hid the ugly underbelly of secrets we were all keeping and sweeping firmly under the mat in case the visitors might see them. Dad hid his bottles of vodka along with the pain of unemployment and uselessness. He was barely visible, a broken shadow, blending into the wallpaper.

'I have nothing to give for you for your wedding,' he said. He wouldn't meet my eyes, but shifted awkwardly from one foot to another, his hands in his pockets playing with his change.

'It doesn't matter,' I said.

His eyes filled with tears and he grabbed my hand. The knobbles of arthritis were already evident in his weak grip.

'I'm sorry,' he said. And somehow, I knew it was for everything, but at the time I didn't understand that forgiveness would have been a gift to myself rather than to him. 'Take any record you want. You know them all.'

On the shelves, the spines of the rarities flashed at me like beacons on a stormy night. He hadn't pawned them yet. I could hear his slight intake of breath as my finger paused over them. I could choose the jewel, Paul Robeson's 1941.

I could take it away again and hide it, to save it from him, to stop him drinking its beauty and pissing it away. Would that make me his saviour? Or would I somehow be beholden, owning and maybe even flaunting his most precious on my own shelf?

I passed it by. I thought I heard him exhale his relief.

I wanted the man from the sunny room to walk me up the aisle. Before he became the flawed man who I adored and raged against in equal measure. That day, though, he was the man who offered me the greatest gift, the only thing he had left of any value.

I took the one that I treasured most, *Harry*.

Dublin, 2012

Ten years after Dad's death, I sat with the last bundle of 78s, 33s and 45s on the floor. Mam hadn't wanted any of them, so my siblings and I had divided them up, and these were my selection. Now they gathered dust, uncatalogued and unplayed. I hadn't even stored them properly. I clung to the guilt of their neglect, because once I let that go, what would I have left? If his record is no longer played, does its music even exist any more?

I offered them to RTÉ for their archives.

'Is there anything of value?' they asked.

Was there?

'No.'

Everything worth anything had been parted with for a cheap bottle, providing Dad with what he needed for a few hours of oblivion.

I had curated these records long enough – a lifetime. I grabbed them and dumped them all into a skip, along with broken furniture and old clothes, covering them over quickly before I changed my mind.

I woke up in the night and looked out through the window. The corner of B1509 was peeping out from under the tarpaulin. He would have known which recording that was, but I didn't know. They were *his* records, after all, not mine.

Dad's records were finally gone, but his music was carved into us all, in an interrupted groove, skipping from one track to the next, still seducing us with memories. Sometimes when we take a small step towards repairing the broken shards, it is into that groove that we drop the needle.

Dublin, 2021

I own one record. ALP 650. *Harry.*

MY BODY FOR HIS

Jessica Moxham

My son Ben had been ill for a week, off school and snotty, but we weren't that concerned about him. If anything, we thought he was improving. It was only when he was suddenly sick during Sunday lunch and then struggling to breathe that we, my husband James and I, got really worried and drove him to A&E.

A nurse quickly put him on a monitor, which confirmed his oxygen levels were low and his heart rate was high. A few hours later his heart was still beating too fast, he needed oxygen to supplement the air around him and he had a fever. He wasn't going home that day. We were in a small room in Paediatric Majors. A nurse had moved out a huge armchair so Ben's wheelchair could fit in there with us. Ben was lying on the bed, grey and uncharacteristically still. His cerebral palsy means his limbs are normally in near constant motion, a whirl of involuntary movements that can be little vibrations or powerful kicks. This usually makes keeping him on a hospital bed a challenge, but not that day. He doesn't talk – he has never talked – but the sounds he was making were hoarse and miserable. A technician brought a mobile X-ray unit in and I left the room while James held Ben still, wearing a tabard made of lead.

A doctor came and told us Ben had an infection: he would need intravenous antibiotics and an oxygen mask.

I stayed until it was dark and then walked home to put our other two children, Max and Molly, to bed. They had been with Ben's carer all afternoon, and had lots of questions about their brother. I sat with them patiently, answering their queries, calming their fears, though I couldn't tell them everything would be OK because Ben had never had to be rushed to hospital before like this.

At 6 a.m. the next morning my dad came to the house so I could return to the hospital. Ben had been moved to a ward. James had a camp bed wedged next to Ben's bed, surrounded by the pleated blue curtains of the small bay. When we packed the bed away there was room for a chair, and I sat holding Ben's hand. It glowed red from the SATs monitor wrapped around his finger. There were other children with their parents on all sides, and James had spent the night vigilantly watching Ben, trying to keep him calm enough to not disturb others, while being kept awake by patients and nurses. Neither of them had slept much. James went home to nap, and I read to Ben. The book we were halfway through was about a boy in hospital, dying of cancer, so I swapped to a gentler story about a group of sisters with no medical conditions.

A nurse came to connect the cannula in Ben's other hand to a bag of clear liquid, but it would not flow. Ben hadn't eaten or drunk for years: we would normally put food and water through his feeding tube, but since we arrived in A&E he had been 'nil by mouth', which actually meant 'nil by stomach', and he was meant to be hydrated through intravenous fluids. But the cannula had failed and he was dry – his lips starting to crack, his skin dull. I carried on reading, wiping his face with a damp cloth. I changed his pyjamas and put cream on his chapped cheeks.

Ben's coughs were weak, and didn't sound to me like they were clearing any of the congestion that was hinted at in his X-ray. I knew it would be better for him to be upright, not lying horizontal as he had been for almost twenty-four hours. He couldn't sit on his own and, at thirteen years old, was too big to sit on my lap. He was too heavy for me to lift into his wheelchair, and there wasn't room for a hoist to help. So instead of moving Ben out of the bed, I pulled on his arms until his chest lifted and climbed behind him. I knelt up, crossing Ben's legs for him and holding his shoulders with my hands. Even in a weakened state, he was moving, and I resisted his attempts to lie back or flop forward. The adjustments were constant and reassuring. His stillness the day before had been terrifying.

Sitting up, his cough was more resonant, and more likely to be shifting the blockades in his bronchioles. I used my palm to slap his back the way a physiotherapist once showed me. Ben has always liked the feeling of being bashed, therapeutically, in this way. He has always enjoyed the sensation of pressure on his body, of my body against his.

I could feel my lower back straining with the effort of keeping him up, but I ignored it for a while – his health is more important than my comfort. Eventually I did lower him back down, sliding him over to one side of the bed so I could lie next to him and hold a book above our heads to read.

The parts of Ben's brain that communicate with his muscles were damaged when he was born, so parts of his body will for ever be just beyond his control. He has always had lots of appointments with doctors. Hours with therapists. Since he was a baby, I have moved Ben's body with him and for him – first in and out of chairs, buggies and beds, later between wheelchairs, standing frames and changing tables. I have helped him open his hands to touch jelly, leant over his cot to hold his arms still so he could get to sleep and lifted him into trees.

Ben can't say that he is thirsty, or move his body into a better position for coughing or tell us he is in pain. He can answer yes if we specifically ask if he's sore, but only if we think to ask the right question. It's up to us to interpret what he needs and how he feels, to help him do these things. I know from the speed and jerkiness of the movement of his back whether he's in pain or bored. I know how tight his hamstrings are and how to make him comfortable in his wheelchair. I can persuade his stiff arm into a coat sleeve.

My body has always been there to help his. In all the unexpectedness and emotional turmoil of having a disabled child, physically helping him has always been the most straightforward part. I carried him and the equipment he needed. When he was three, I got pregnant again and kept lifting Ben until the week before I gave birth. When that baby, Max, was born I put him in a sling in order to have my hands free to push Ben's wheelchair.

Shortly before Molly was born, when Ben was five, a new occupational therapist came to our house. She listened to me describe our bathing routine: carrying Ben into the bathroom and placing him on a mesh hammock on top of the bath, pulling a handle to lower him into the water, picking him up again. She said I should stop doing this immediately. It was very bad for our backs, and an unacceptable thing to ask paid carers to do. We would have to bed-bath Ben until we could adapt our bathroom. I said I thought the feeling of his unpredictable body being in warm water was one of Ben's great joys, but she was unmoved and uninterested. I made sure she never had anything to do with my family again and carried on lifting Ben.

It was only after Molly turned one that the years of growing babies and then carrying them caught up with me. I started to feel my lower back ache when I carried her. My left hip hurt when I carried baskets of washing and when I lifted Ben into his bed. One morning I was woken by an insistence in my spine, and when I tried to sit up I yelped in pain. The searing crisis across my lower back was shocking. When I called the GP there were no appointments. James did everything for the kids that morning while I cried. Every time I moved I was on fire. It was inconceivable that I could be like this for long, and I got a doctor's appointment when I called again.

James took me to the surgery and I walked slowly, holding on to him, standing in the waiting area because sitting felt too risky. When I saw the nurse I said that the pain was the same as childbirth, expecting this to convey the severity of it, but she seemed unimpressed. She prescribed a muscle relaxant and painkillers. I waited in the rain while James went into the pharmacy, and then I took the tablets right there on the pavement, looking to the grey sky on the side of a busy road, hoping they would make it bearable.

The tablets did help. My back was still very, very painful but I didn't feel as helpless or consumed. I visited a chiropractor and applied ice packs. I saw a physio and diligently did the little exercises she showed me. I couldn't do anything for my family for a week, and even then I could stand to cook but not lift, cuddle or change them. Max and Molly came and saw me in my room – Max returning from school and showing me a drawing, Molly toddling over to the side of the bed. James carried Ben up to see me, holding him on his lap so I could ask about his day, while putting on a brave face.

Over the next few years it happened again and again – painful enough to stop me being able to look after the kids, do the things I wanted to or work, but not as bad as the first time. I developed nerve pain, which sent tingles and aches down my legs. For months I had to leave earlier than usual to collect Max from school because I could only walk slowly. I was exhausted from the whole-body tension waves of a sciatic nerve in distress.

In Pilates classes I started to visualise how the muscles at the front of my body connected with those at the back. How they were all meant to be keeping my spine aligned, taut, held. 'Think of your back as a string of pearls and move each bead separately,' I was told – but my lumbar region was more an iron rod than a necklace. When a doctor showed me a scan on a computer screen I could see each vertebra, with the pale ribbon of the spinal canal running through them from top to bottom. Darker patches between the bones were soft discs, and four of them were bulging out beyond their usual boundaries. One formed a neat circle beyond the bone. It was the closest thing I could see to a pearl, but the herniated discs were putting pressure on the nerves that ran through the cavity in the middle, which was causing the pain. The bundle of nerves in the spinal canal – the 'horse tail' – could become squashed to the point of being permanently damaged, he said. Be careful.

Over the next five years I had periods where my back was so persistently painful that I was impatient and sharp with my children. I started to use a hoist to lift Ben, rather than doing it myself. I felt the lengthening of his limbs and the stiffness that made them hard to bend, but I still had to change him, help settle him in bed, interpret what he thought and wanted. When I read Molly her bedtime story I sat, gingerly, on the edge of her bed and asked her to turn off her moon-shaped light because I couldn't bend down to the switch. Max stopped asking me to go on the trampoline with him.

Sometimes I was pain-free and able to do what I needed to. I pushed Ben in his wheelchair with ease, though always with care. I leant over the bath to wash Max's hair, and sat on the floor to build towers with Molly. I had moments of full, wholehearted appreciation for my body's ability to move and relax. But it only took a moment, or an unremarkable sequence of events, to throw it off again.

Six months before Ben was admitted to hospital, I had been in Copenhagen for the weekend to watch James and my sister Maddy run a marathon. Ben stayed at home with his granny, but Max and Molly were there with their cousins and Maddy's partner George. At the finish line, George and I stuffed pieces of ham into slices of bread for the kids while we waited to see Maddy and James. Runners streamed past, looking jubilant or broken – extraordinary displays of physical endurance. Maddy came past first, concentrating so much that she almost didn't see us. Half an hour later we saw James coming down the straight, and George helped Max vault the barrier to join him. They crossed the finish line together, James getting a little burst of energy from Max's company. By the time they joined us on a patch of grass, surrounded by other runners and their families, popping Champagne and eating ice creams, James and Maddy had regained their breath and were tired but joyous.

'You did it!' we all cried, as Molly and her cousin Ralph stole their medals, and Maddy's son Arnie pottered off towards a dog poo.

We had another day in Copenhagen being tourists, eating at restaurants, visiting playgrounds. As I got out of bed on our final morning, leaning over to pack my suitcase, I could feel that my back had not appreciated the soft hotel bed. I lay on the floor and stretched. On the flight I couldn't get comfortable in the seat and put my hand behind me, pushing against the sore bit, trying to ease the developing ache.

By the time we got off the flight and began the long walk from the gate to the main terminal, I knew things were really bad. My lower back was ablaze, and I could feel all of the muscles around being drawn into the flames. I held my hips with my hands, trying to brace it all together, but nothing helped. The pain was so sudden it made me cry, and I stopped, leaning against a rail as James told the others to go on ahead. As I slowly walked again, the vision in my right eye went blurry, so I knew I might faint. As we stood in the passport queue I did my best impression of someone who wasn't about to collapse, and when we got through to the other side James went to find a wheelchair. Sitting was slightly less painful than walking, and definitely faster. Max and Molly looked at me warily.

We had done this journey before with Ben, so James knew to find someone to show us the step-free route. A man who worked for the train company took command of my wheelchair, showing us the way. Molly came next to me in the lift and held my hand. I was bumped along the bobbly platform, the man shouting at people to get out of our way. I was tensed in the chair, my arms tight on the armrests to absorb the shocks. I thought, I must remember what this feels like the next time I am pushing Ben over uneven ground.

On the train I breathed deeply and concentrated completely on surviving the journey. At Victoria, James found a taxi which I scrunched myself into. Max and Molly were watchful, their quiet compliance unusual. I knew they were worried about me. At home I walked, extremely slowly, up to the door, through to the lift that Ben normally used, up to my bedroom and, with another lightening shot of searing pain, lowered myself down on to my bed with relief that at least I didn't have to move for a while.

I couldn't get a doctor's appointment until the following morning, and I calculated that it would be at least nineteen hours until I could get medication prescribed. James rummaged in our medicine box and found some expired painkillers that I took, but which didn't help. Moving to sit on the edge of my bed, then to stand, required a steeling of mind over matter. I tensed in anticipation of the agony. Once upright I gripped on to the windowsill, breathing in through my nose and out through my mouth slowly, rhythmically, like

35

I did when I was in labour with Ben. Then I had wondered if I would survive the pain, and I had. I asked James what the noise was outside, but it was static in my own ears telling me I might faint.

James brought Ben up to see me. He wheeled Ben round to my side of the bed and we told him about how I had used a wheelchair in the airport, which Ben found funny.

Molly was not at all amused. 'You were a weird colour, Mummy. Like, completely white.'

That night James slept on the floor of our bedroom. He had seen me like this many times before – previous back spasms, post-childbirth, post-surgery – and he was solicitous and sympathetic, bringing me food, helping me put on my pants, getting a straw when I couldn't tip my head to drink – looking after me in all the ways I would usually help Ben.

I couldn't arrange words in a way that felt like an accurate description of the pain, and I was terrified I wouldn't be believed. I knew I sounded like I could be exaggerating, almost hysterical, which is how I felt. I wasn't sure I could survive this level of agony for much longer. When I got through to the doctor's surgery in the morning, all of the appointments had gone. What do I do? I asked the receptionist. I filled in a form online, as she suggested, trying to walk a line between hyperbole and reality.

A doctor, who I had known since I was Molly's age, called later that morning. He asked me legitimate, practical questions and prescribed relaxants and strong painkillers. James was standing at the window of our bedroom, and the look of relief on his face must have mirrored my own. He immediately left for the chemist. There was hope.

Within an hour of taking the tablets, I felt the spasm begin to ease. In the mirror, my torso was asymmetrical – one side up against my arm, the other curved with a big gap. As Ben's physios were always telling us, you want the body to be as symmetrical as possible, and mine wasn't even close.

After about three weeks I was almost pain-free and more balanced. I could walk and feed Ben. I could put Molly to bed, and resented having to lean over to pick discarded clothes up off the floor even more than usual. I applied ice packs, took weaker painkillers and lay on my back on the floor, tentatively bringing my knee to my chest to stretch, sliding a tennis ball under my glute to press into the muscle. My torso slowly untwisted and I carried on with my life, grateful to be able to care for my children again and not have to be cared for.

In the hospital with Ben, a doctor came to put a new cannula in the back of his other hand. She got the needle ready while a nurse and I held Ben down. She tried three times, Ben's body bucking every time, but wasn't able to get the needle in the right place. Ben cried and eventually she gave up. I put on an audiobook, hoping he would get lost in a story, and tried not to cry. Ben coughed, unproductively. His mouth would usually be wet with saliva, pushed out by a tongue that is in constant motion, but he was so dry. I held his warm hands, kissed him on the forehead, drank some water myself, then got back on to the bed, balancing Ben's shoulders between my hands, splaying my legs either side of his. I straightened him when he started to bend, and pulled him back towards me when he began to slide away. James found us like this when he pulled aside the blue curtain. After kissing Ben on the forehead, saying he looked a bit better, he said to me that I should be careful of my back.

Maybe my back gets sore because I spent years lifting Ben, holding him and supporting his body in ways it cannot support itself. I lent my body to his when he needed my help, and to my other children too – carrying them inside my womb, then in my arms. I flexed over them as they breastfed, picked them up when they cried and lifted them into climbing frames that were too tall. I have spent years bending over Ben's body to keep it as supple as it can be, as symmetrical as possible. I have stretched his hamstrings and encouraged him to strengthen his neck muscles. Now I do these things to myself too – stretching my glutes, building up the network of muscles that should support my spine. Sometimes when I am doing Pilates exercises I can feel the part of my lower abdomen which was sewn back together, twice, after Max and Molly were born and has felt slightly unfamiliar ever since. What I have done for them is a part of me. I should resent the toll this has taken.

Perhaps I have all the pain because of those children. Yet when I'm incapacitated, or curtailing what I do, I don't resent them, I just hate not being able to help them. Sometimes Molly says, 'Mama, stand here, like this,' and she mimes legs apart, arms open wide. She runs away from me, then turns and sprints back towards me full pelt. If my back isn't hurting, I catch her, swing her up and round in a full turn before putting her back down. When my mum sees me doing this she tells me off, because we all know it could injure me, but I love it. My problem is only partly that I can't control my

38

body and its internal pulls and pushes. I'm also not willing to control it because I want to touch and care for my kids. I want and need to help Ben move and cough. It doesn't feel like a sacrifice.

On the third day of Ben's hospital stay he is much better. Still coughing, and on antibiotics, but well enough for us to monitor him at home. Max and Molly come to the hospital with James and find us in a new bay, big enough for Ben to be in his wheelchair next to the bed. There's football on the TV, and while we wait to be discharged Max lies back on the bed, spilling crisps on the sheets, while Molly sits on the arm of Ben's wheelchair. They have been quietly, extremely worried and are happy to be with their brother again. I sit on a chair, looking at them all. We'll all be home soon and I'll take care of them. I'd do it all again. I will carry on doing it if I can. All the lifting, carrying and worrying. I give it all gladly – the time, the care and the integrity of the soft cushions of tissue between the bones of my spine.

NO THANKS!

Sheena Hussain

Cancer and carer – talk about a double whammy! Or is it a hat trick? I'm also celibate. Mind you, not by choice – well, sort of. I mean, how does one even muster the energy after cancer to start fishing for a potential suitor? Did I mention my daily marathons of disposing soiled Tena pads ten times a day? Ah, yes, my mama dearest – I'm her non-paid carer and I live with her in this bungalow.

A suitor for me is a husband, not a boyfriend, partner or anything in between. Yes, you guessed right – I'm a Muslim; our culture is somewhat more conservative than yours, which means we can't try before we buy.

Yes, Islam – that barbaric religion that the media tries to sell you actually offers you choice. Don't look so shocked. I'm allowed to say no. If he looks like or has the mannerisms of Mr Bean, never mind religion – I think any sane woman would say, NO THANKS!

It's hard looking after Mama at times. It takes up all the God-given hours – there's rarely any time for me. I can't remember the last time I had one of those deluxe rejuvenating facials, and my feet are looking a tad withered, with cracks around the heels. I mean, a girl wants to look her best when she's trying to 'pull herself a husband'. Don't stand a chance, do I – well, against those women. I mean, look at them: fluttery eyelashes, bleached teeth, nails all prim and proper. Cinderella won't be going to the ball for a long time yet, I can tell you, and that's a fact.

It's been a few years now since the cancer. When I was first diagnosed I was given all that 'soft talk' by the consultant – like a lottery ball holding the winnings, I was meant to be grateful that I got the 'better cancer'. They never tell you what life will really be like: the side effects, fatigue, dry skin, brain fog (or 'cancer brain', as I like to call it) – the list goes on and on.

It's rubbish if you ask me – how is my cancer any different to breast cancer? I've not had a breast removed, but I've had my thyroid gland 'stolen' from me – well, part of it. I say 'stolen' because I still feel they shouldn't have removed the left lobe. They were concerned it was cancer; turned out it wasn't. I wear the scar of two lots of surgery. I mean, I'm no different to a woman with breast cancer, right? Just like her, I too wonder daily and try to comprehend: What if it comes back a second time?

Strange, isn't it, how we put complete trust in these medical people – as if they were gods! Well, they aren't. I regret not doing more research. But it's done with; there's no going back now.

It was my birthday a few days ago: forty-two; that makes me an 'adult child', still living with my mother. That means I've been with her the longest. I don't know how I've survived. We have good days and bad days between us; she has a lot of flatulence (gastro problems) and I mainly laugh. A great combination – I bet that's why God put us together.

We have a strict routine. I yank the bed sheets off her at 6 a.m.… Calm down – I'm joking! I'm not that cruel. Here's a thought – if I hadn't pursued a career in law, I would have made a damn good recruit in the navy. I have all the qualities: early riser, impeccable organisation skills and masterfully disciplined.

'Wakey-wakey, Mama, it's 8.00 a.m. – time to get up! Rise and shine!'

She looks at me stoically, clutching her duvet close to her chin; I know beneath the visage she is cursing me in my mother tongue.

I wish she'd get up same time as me. I mean, who wants to do two breakfasts? It's just not economical, especially not now with the cost of living swinging like an axe ready to kill us all. I like to air the room as soon as she gets up. The smell of faeces overnight can't be good for her lungs. She's stopped using the adapted raised toilet in her wet room. Besides, it's not flushing. Problem with the electrics. I called for a quote the other day – £300! I couldn't believe it. Where do you think she keeps that kind of money – under her mattress? I said to myself. I told him I'm still shopping around for quotes, said a swift goodbye and put the phone down on him.

It's on my to-do list, when I get around to it. She's more often than not on the commode; it sits close to her bedside like it's her best friend.

I sometimes hear her talking to it – or maybe it's just her babbling whilst she sits on it; not that you are meant to talk while doing either No. 1 or No. 2 if you are a Muslim.

It's seen as bad etiquette. Oh, and just for the record, we don't just wipe – we wash with water. Now, you see, that's where the western world is going wrong, if you ask me: poor bathroom manners. Just look at what they did during the lockdown. Patronising, telling us to wash our hands – well, some of us wash our backsides each and every time nature calls. I struggled those early months, just me and her, no outside help, not even from my siblings. We played by the rules – unlike some.

'Have you made my breakfast?' she asks. 'I'm hungry…'

'Er, just a moment, Mama, I'm on the bloody phone to the nurse – she wants to come and do your bloods, and if you had woken up two hours earlier you could have had a warm breakfast, same time as me, so I'm sorry, but it's just cornflakes with cold milk for you, young lady.'

She tucks her head under the duvet like a sulking child. I'm not sure if it's because I won the argument over breakfast, or if the thought of nurses coming to squeeze blood out terrorises her.

She doesn't like giving blood. I mean, who does? Avoids it like the plague if she can. But she has to, every three months, due to a strong rheumatism arthritis drug that she takes – I can't remember the name; she won't be given the pills otherwise. She's no skin left – all dry bone – it's eaten years off her.

A few months back they tried to pick her vein from the crease of the elbow – she's always creased from there: she can't bend it; they know that. On this occasion I agreed with her when she called them 'stupid cows'.

Causing her all that distress – there was no need. The aftermath is no fun, either. She has to sleep with purple bruises and I have to witness them – to think in her prime she had beautiful supple collagen in her skin. I can picture her in Lister Park in the bandstand, balancing my sister – younger than me – on her pelvic bone, fair skinned and glowing in the sun.

People come and visit her now and they say, 'I bet she was beautiful in her youth – you can still see it in those hazel eyes.'

I guess she was, and that's why my father married her.

She's far from beautiful when she screams at me. Occasionally, I sit in the lounge whilst she is in her adapted room. There are no floors to separate us, just thin walls. Maybe I do hear her, but sometimes I just zone out, escape and come out of my head, leaving the sounds of wailing and the smell of thick bleach behind.

She swears in my mother tongue – there's no point repeating it; you wouldn't understand anyway, and I would be sinning. I don't want God's wrath to fall upon me twice: once for not responding to her call, and a second time for swearing – NO THANKS!

Some days I wish I wasn't celibate – maybe being married means you can go off and enjoy your life, not having to worry about caring for the old. There are seven of us – that includes me. Don't get me wrong, my siblings help out whenever they can, but the bulk of it falls on me. Well, it makes sense, as I'm the one who lives with her. They don't see the daily grind, the nitty-gritty, her sobbing as she tries to get herself off to sleep.

Growing up in my culture, I was always taught the eldest son is responsible for his mother's care. Somehow they passed this off as religion – you know, Sharia law. Well, to be honest, I do find it a little odd. Why would Allah place the entire burden on one child? It didn't make sense to me. When I grew up and looked into it for myself I learnt it's more to do with proximity – for the child who lives closest the duty of care increases. So, by way of example, let's say if our T lived over in America (over his dead body), his duty to Mama wouldn't be as great as mine, who lives in the same house as her. Do you see my point? Anyway, we're all from the same womb, which makes us equal, so why wouldn't we all want to serve her?

Moving into the bungalow was a nightmare in itself. Making sure we picked every last disabled homemade gadget, like the drawstring she used to slip her socks on. In my mother-tongue you call it a *naada*, used by elders instead of elastic to keep their trousers up. I remember having a conversation about this in her bedroom, in the old house, at Number 238.

'Well, I would rather have elastic – at least that way the knot is secure. I mean, can you imagine, Mama, a loose shoelace knot that came undone – you'd be wearing your bloody shalwar around your ankles! OK, if you're an old woman, I'm a young lady, and sometimes I fall behind with waxing my legs… have some decorum, Mama – NO THANKS!'

'No, silly girl, it's all in the knot,' she explained.

'Well, what about when you need to go to the toilet urgently? I'm not fussing over a clove hitch/bowline/ sheet bend or whatever. I want to go in and do my business and out. Who's going to carry a bodkin with them in case the drawstring suddenly decides to play hide and seek from its hem?'

'You girls – anything for a quick and easy life!' she chimed in.

It's probably why I still don't wear the traditional two-piece shalwar kameez as often as I should even today. The thought of it coming down with a good old fashion *naada* would send me to an early grave.

Back in her prime she'd wear hers elegantly. The soft pastel colours suited her fair skin. She's not bothered what she wears these days, as long as it's comfortable. Most often you'll find her in a loose nightie, and on a good day she will be in her traditional 'two-piecer' – the old scruffy ones which smell of mustard oil. She's had them for years; doesn't seem to want to let go. Maybe holding on is a way of surviving – a piece of her culture, her homeland, her memories.

She doesn't talk to me about marriage any more. We just don't discuss it.

Yesterday the community nurses were here. Different ones come and go. The ones that came this last time took me by surprise. They had come to check Mama's bed sores and to see if she needed any equipment. I was finding a letter for them to chase the occupational therapy department at the Council. You see, she needs an adapted chair to sit on – it pains me that she sits on the hard shower chair. She can't lower herself on to and lift herself off the cream recliner we bought her. They told us she was top priority; it will be a year in March they've done absolutely nothing. Not even a phone call to update us – zero communication.

It's criminal if you ask me.

'How are you, Sheena? How are you coping? Do you need anything?' She just came out with it. Took me by complete surprise, I didn't know how to feel. No one has asked me in a long while how I am, as a carer, whether I am coping. It was very kind of her.

I wanted to tell her the truth, but I'm my mother's daughter – I kept a stiff upper lip, I smiled and said, 'I'm absolutely fine.'

The reality is that carers live a concealed life – until we come out of the bubble no one will know the invisible truth but us.

By the way, did I mention I'm a poet now? I write whenever I get time. She's ambling about in her room – I'm going to see if I can write a few lines before I'm called back through.

PALMISTRY

Kerry Mead

Picture a moment when time stretches – a pause suspended. It could be placed in any slow, late-summer afternoon in rural England in the past fifty years or so. A young girl is sitting head down at a polished walnut dining table in her grandparents' living room, fully absorbed in what she is doing. She's surrounded by books, sketch pads, pencils and pens. Dust motes are hanging and spinning in the sunlight streaming through the window behind her; the heavy silence punctuated and intensified by the tick of the carriage clock on the mantelpiece.

She puts her pen down on the walnut table, looks up and raises her hands in front of her face to study them. She turns her right hand around slowly, fingers splayed, palm facing away. The back of her hand is tanned, plump and smooth, springy to the touch. There's one large tawny freckle about two inches below the point where her index and middle finger meet. She carries on scrutinising her hands for some time, comparing the two with deep intent, her brow furrowed, wiggling her fingers, touching her thumb tips together. The girl brings them down again with a small smile – a smile of 'yes, I told you so'. She turns her attention back to what she was doing before. The clock continues ticking. The dust motes begin their dance again.

≈

Picture a different moment with the same plasticity, a similarly late-summer afternoon, but you're not in sleepy rural England now; you're in the middle of a city. Another girl of the same age sits head down at a kitchen table singing to herself as she kneads and shapes a lump of clay, surrounded by tubes of paint, jars of brushes, pens and palette knives. She wants to be an *artist* when she grows up. Or maybe a *writer.*

As the sunlight cuts in through the open window and slices across the wall to the side of her, the sound of the radio playing in the background fades away. Her busy fingers and dimpled knuckles continue moving rhythmically. The girl stops to inspect her work whilst absent-mindedly rubbing at the smears of clay drying and cracking on her hands. She frowns – she doesn't look entirely pleased with what she sees. She picks up her palette knife and starts sculpting as the music on the radio starts up again.

≈

I stop typing, raise my head and look around me. I'm alone in the house sitting at my desk facing out onto the back garden. I bring my hands up in front of my face to study them, rotating them slowly from front to back. It still feels like a luxury to pause and look at my hands for as long as I want. I lightly trace my right index finger along the lines that thread across my left palm and let my mind wander.

When my oldest was born the *I* who had time to stop and stare at her hands split away from the *I* who then became *Mum/Mummy/Mother/She*. My past self was many things I'm not now, and part of that past self, the *Ich* of the Romantics, was being an *artist*, a *writer*. This new *I*, *Mum/Mummy/ Mother/She*, felt so natural and easy to slip into by the time I had my first child. I didn't realise I'd been losing my creative *I* until it was long gone. It was like deciding one morning to take off a ring which I had been wearing every day for years and placing it somewhere for safekeeping, then much later realising with a pang of horror it wasn't in my possession any more, and having no idea exactly where or when I lost it.

Then I forgot about the lost ring completely when I became a single mother. The following decade was one where life was lived in firefighting mode, purely in the present tense: *wake-up-Mummy-out-of-bed-make-breakfast-drive-to-school-drive-to-work-work-work-work-sit-in-traffic-pick-up-the-kids-drive-home-tea-bath-story-time-bed.*

In *Mothers: An Essay on Love and Cruelty*, Jacqueline Rose considers Simone de Beauvoir's existential assertion that to truly live you must be free to shape your own life without impediment. For de Beauvoir 'the woman trapped in her home cannot found her existence for herself.'[1] De Beauvoir presents a stark choice for women between culture and nature; if you choose the creation of babies you give up the space in your life for the creation of anything else.

During this period of single parenthood I was not trapped in my home, but I *was* trapped in a life of providing

---

1 Jacqueline Rose, *Mothers: An Essay on Love and Cruelty* (London: Faber and Faber, 2018), p. 133.

for my children. If bringing up two young children alone and then collapsing into bed each night with no time for even one roaming thought before you pass out is an act of constant firefighting, then you can only find time to breathe again once the blaze starts receding. Only then can you hear the angry cry of 'FUCK IT WHAT ABOUT *ME*?' rising from the smouldering ashes and the gaping wound of your broken heart. Only when the firefighting stage was over could I stretch time and start thinking in the past and future tenses again. Only then could I begin to answer that cry and resume the work of founding my own existence.

The spectres of mother-artists haunt me now that I have realised the importance of what I gave up so easily. Sylvia Plath, Audre Lorde, Alice Walker – their words and actions taunt me in moments of self-doubt. These women obstinately carved out space for the *I* they couldn't fully exist without after becoming mothers. All of this was achieved in seemingly direct opposition to de Beauvoir's insistence that choosing motherhood and domesticity must mean the certain death of cultural production. Maybe they had guts I don't possess, and this is what haunts me.

When I am sitting at my desk tracing the lines on my palms, that is when the girl sitting at the walnut table emerges in front of me, fresh and vivid – a released muscle memory. Our *I*s overlap again for a moment; an echo that quickens my heart. We are both writing a story.

The girl stops writing, puts her pen down on the table and raises her hands to study them again. She looks closer and notices the middle finger and thumb of her right hand are a different shape to the left. She touches the tips of her two thumbs together and holds them up in front of her face. There is a dent on the inner edge of her right thumb below the middle knuckle. The dent is from playing the clarinet – it is where her right thumb rests under the flat silver hook attached to the back of the instrument, leaving the rest of her fingers to flow freely over the tone holes and bridge keys.

Holding her right hand up again to re-examine the dent in her thumb, her gaze drifts up to a rough bump on the left-hand side of her middle finger, just above the top knuckle. There is a sweeping hollow below it: a home for pencils and felt-tip pens. The girl would regularly examine her hands in quiet moments after this. After she'd confirmed the dents, bumps and hollows were still there, she would smile to herself and continue with whatever she was doing. Or she would unconsciously rub the callous on the side of her middle finger when lost deep in thought, or as she fell asleep. Rubbing it gently over and over with the pad of her thumb, observing its roughness, pressing it harder until she could feel the bony protrusion growing underneath, a secret nugget of warmth, the knowledge that she can shape her own hands, shape her own future, sparking deep inside her.

I want her back.

≈

'Mum. MUM. Can we draw together?'

Ava is my youngest. My daughter. Her favourite thing to do with me is to sit alongside each other and draw. She wants to be an *artist* when she grows up, or maybe a *writer*. I think she likes to draw alongside me because she has my full attention, but there is none of the usual mum-and-daughter push and pull; we are just sharing the same space. When we draw together side by side in silence our hands are in gentle conversation. I like to glance over at her when she is concentrating and won't notice me looking. I know that sometimes she glances over at me as well.

I look up from my laptop.

'OK, let's draw in a bit. Give me five minutes.'

Then I remember I've been thinking about doing something for a while.

'Can I draw your hand?'

She looks at me aslant.

'You know I'm writing about hands at the moment? Well, I want to illustrate it. I want to draw a picture of my hand when I was about your age, and your hand looks just like mine did then.'

She shrugs.

'OK.'

We sit next to each other at the living room table. I ask her to position her right hand flat on the table, then I start to sketch it. I sharpen a pencil and smooth over the paper in front of me. She is fidgety, squirming in her seat, but she keeps her right hand perfectly still. Using her free hand to unlock her phone she starts watching a video on YouTube. I haven't looked at her hands in detail for a long time – probably since she was a toddler, when sometimes I would gently uncurl her loose fists as she slept next to me and trace the tiny lines on her palms in wonder. I admire her smooth skin and dimpled knuckles as I draw. Tiny flakes of pale-grey clay are stuck in her cuticles, but I don't include them in my sketch. I was never much of a sculptor.

'There. I'm nearly done.'

She looks up from her phone and frowns.

'Mum. MUM, it's so good! Hands are so hard! Why can't I draw hands like that?'

I lean back in my chair to observe the finished sketch.

'Just one more thing.'

I pick up my pencil and quickly stamp a freckle on the back of the hand. A full stop.

'There.'

I sit back to admire my work.

'Mum. I don't have a freckle on my hand!'

'But I do. It's meant to be my hand.'

It's only then I feel a stab of something – a precise incision of shame running straight through my gut. Now that she has her hand back Ava starts drawing her own version of it, and I carry on with mine, not showing any outward sign of the gnawing of guilt starting its slow crawl up my spine. Making my mark on my daughter, claiming my territory. I try to concentrate on my sketch, but the lines swim in front of me. I feel like I've crossed a boundary I promised myself I never would – not with *my* daughter. If in the future she finds out how much I want to possess her she might leave me – slam the door behind her and never come back.

≈

When we carry our children in our bodies there is an element of ownership – their body is a part of ours. In the early twenty-first century the concept of a fourth trimester of pregnancy started to be commonly discussed in parenting books and antenatal classes. In 2013 the medical writer Susan Brink wrote:

> A newborn human is not so much a baby as a final-phase fetus living through a time of transition as he gives up the comforts of the uterus and gradually adjusts to the wonders and challenges of the world. Further, during this period infants and mothers need to stay almost as tightly bound together as biology dictated during the first three trimesters.[2]

---

2 Susan Brink, *The Fourth Trimester: Understanding, Protecting, and Nurturing an Infant Through the First Three Months* (Berkeley, USA: University of California Press, 2013), p. 14. http://ebookcentral.proquest.com/lib/bbk/detail.action?docID=1187672

The barrier between the self and the other is at its flimsiest in the first week after your child is born. You have been on a grand adventure together. You both stared death in the face. You couldn't have done it without each other. You lie together and bleed together in the days after birth/labour as you ease your breast into their open, grasping mouth:

> Like the act of reproduction, lactation is the enactment of a splitting, of a formation of self and part-self that is to become other. It disrupts the dominant motif of the bounded body, of sovereign individuality. Milk is a bridge between bodies: an emission from one and incorporation into another.[3]

Hormones have a bridging role in this corporeal blurring as well, leaching from the mother into the baby's body in utero. Around 4–5% of female newborns menstruate in the days directly after birth, and around the same percentage of newborns, both male and female, produce their own neonatal milk, commonly called witch's milk.[4][5] The term 'witch's milk' is borrowed from ancient folklore, in which

3 Esther Leslie and Melanie Jackson, 'Milk's Arrays', *Studies in the Maternal, Queer Milk*, 10.1 (2018), p. 16. https://www.mamsie.bbk.ac.uk/article/id/4276/

4 Paola Bianchi, Giuseppe Benagiano and Ivo Brosens, 'Promoting Awareness of Neonatal Menstruation', *Gynecological Endocrinology*, 33.3 (2017), 173–78. https://doi.org/10.1080/09513590.2016.1259408

5 D. J. Madlon-Kay, '"Witch's Milk". Galactorrhea in the Newborn', *American Journal of Diseases of Children* (1960), 140.3 (1986), 252–53. https://doi.org/10.1001/archpedi.1986.02140170078035

witches' familiars suckled and gained sustenance at babies' oestrogen-bloated breasts.[6]

Read the parenting books and explore the online forums and you can't help but feel in the modern era it is 'unmotherly' to view any excretion from your newborn's body as disgusting. I remember reading that you should suck your baby's snot out of their nostrils if they catch a cold because they can't blow their own noses. I often felt that if I showed any outward signs of disgust at my baby's corporeality the unseen judge and jury would decide I wasn't a good enough mother. Maybe the fact that I baulked at the thought of ingesting my child's snot could also be a sign I was out of touch with my own animalistic mother-as-self as well.

A good mother relishes getting her hands dirty, being up to her elbows in her baby's piss, shit, blood and vomit. Handle your placenta after you birth it, marvel at it, eat it. Breastfeed on demand. Co-sleep. Carry your child twenty-four-seven. Inhale the smell of their shit and declare it the scent of roses. Forgo all alcohol, nicotine and spicy foods. Be available for your child to access at all times.

Your sense of self can start to come undone when immersed in the fertile loam of the other.

It's then easy to start believing your lost *I* lives on in your child.

The twentieth-century philosopher Emmanuel Levinas believed humankind has an infinite moral responsibility to care for the other, and it is only through coming face to face with the other and recognising this responsibility that

---

6 Thomas R. Forbes, 'Witch's Milk and Witches' Marks', *The Yale Journal of Biology and Medicine*, 22.3 (1950), 219–25.

we can truly experience the subjective *I*. Modern Western thought surrounding the human condition is abundant with theories exploring the concept of the self and the other, but how many of them deal with the maternal self's encounter with the gaze of the other in the face of her child? Very few, even though early motherhood is a perfect example of a time in life when moral responsibility, unconditional love for the other and unclear physical and emotional boundaries are a central part of the human experience.

Ava decides to draw her hand as well. I admire it when she shows it to me.

'Mum. Are you going to use my drawing too?'

'I wasn't going to, but if you want me to I can. It's so good.'

'But it's nowhere near as good as yours.'

That's another thing we share – she is also a perfectionist. I briefly feel a jolt of pleasure that she is so much like me. I push away this thought – dark sustenance for my familiar.

≈

Carrying a child feels like the biggest magic trick in the world. You gaze at the beating blur in front of you at your first scan; later you feel it flutter inside you like it's trying to fly away. It seems like witchcraft, the ultimate act of creativity, like nothing you or anyone else has experienced before. There is magic in labour as well. In the moments before Ava was born I felt like I'd been plunged into a primordial lake, a dark tide, seemingly endless. I could still hear the midwife's voice clearly, but it sounded undulating and far away. I was an opening, an unfurling, on the brink of life and death. My edges dissolved. Different from the knowledge during pregnancy that another body was within mine, now the contained self no longer existed. And from that material, another person was cleaved into being. I had also experienced the same dark tide when my son was dangled in front of me shortly after he was born. The pethidine fug cleared for a split second and a heavy sheet of dark, subaqueous matter crept across the operating theatre and curled around both of us, then retreated as he lifted his head to the lights, legs kicking, screwed up his face and screamed for the first time.

Having been thrust deeply into this state of the apparent infinite and divine, who would want to push away its memory and risk forgetting it for ever? You may never dive into it again, but every time you look at your child out in the world you receive a reminder that it happened, and that the world is not completely rational after all. And then there is the additional ecstasy when the mother looks at her daughter, the knowledge that she has produced a new person in her own image.

I pull my daughter back.

Soon she will start to push me away.

Both the self and the other need space to retreat into the privacy of the *I* as a means of creating a solid self-identity, to exist in the wider world as sure-footedly as possible. Just as the mother discovers on one hand how entangled she and her child are, whether feeding off each other or starving each other, she must also learn, on the other hand, to let her child begin to extricate themself for their own good and, ultimately, hers as well.

It is a push

-pull.

Eventually, the child must reject the mother.

But where does this leave me? What is my future when I've given up my *I*?

≈

On a whim I open up my laptop and Google palm reading, then spend the rest of the morning trying to read my fortune. The site I land on tells me the right palm maps out my present and future, the left my past. After coming to an abrupt end just below my index finger the lifeline on my left palm is hard to distinguish from the mishmash of other crossed lines and broken paths surrounding it. On my right palm my heart line is deep like a cut; my lifeline is long and faint. I can't make sense of my fate here.

I turn my right hand over. It looks very different to what it looked like at my grandparents' walnut table, but it holds the same genetic road maps at cellular level, although the surface terrain has changed. There's the same tawny freckle a couple of inches below the crease between my index and middle finger. It's less prominent than it used to be – it straddles a now-visible tendon, fighting for the eye's attention with a flaking, purplish scar from a recent splash of cooking oil, bright-pink knuckles and greenish veins pushing up from underneath the hand's thinner, more translucent skin.

Holding my thumbs up tip to tip to compare the two, I am surprised to see the ghost of a dent still visible on my right thumb, even though I stopped playing the clarinet thirty years ago. There is a new mark circling the base of the same finger, shiny and pale – the ghost of a ring I always used to wear. My writer's bump is still visible too, but it protrudes less and is smooth now instead of calloused. What do I feel inside as I rub that bump with the pad of my thumb? Warm sparking.

I gaze at the freckle again. That spot holds the past, present and future in its pigment. It remains. An anchoring. I can reshape my hands and even the palm lines can change their direction over time, but that freckle, alongside the dent from playing the clarinet and my writer's bump, is always there. If I took a pen or the handle of a paintbrush and drove it through my flesh and tendons at the site of that tawny mark, it would emerge on the other side exactly halfway along my lifeline, maybe changing its course for ever. I could alter my fate.

I remind myself the freckle is not on Ava's hand, only mine.

≈

Not long afterwards Ava and I cuddle up on the sofa one night to watch TV. Ava reaches out for my hand, holds it in hers and begins examining it closely. She prods the veins on the back of my hand and pinches the skin together, lifting it up and watching it slowly melt back into place when she lets go. Then she starts again. It's like a dance. It makes me feel queasy having my veins and arteries prodded, being subject to her dissecting observations, but I let her do it anyway. Ava's gaze, both through her eyes and hands, others me. To be able to touch anything there must be space between the I and the other; this dance brings into sharp focus this distance between us. The queasiness is brought on by my realisation of this distance. If I don't let her go voluntarily I can only see a future where I am diminished, and she blazes in that otherness.

Recently, difficult mother-daughter relationships keep appearing everywhere around me. As we sit next to each other, her head on my shoulder, her folded legs curled into and mirroring mine, my hand in hers, I think about the closing scene from the book I have just finished. In Deborah Levy's *Hot Milk* Rose (the demanding Mother) and Sofia (the adult daughter and carer with her cries of FUCK IT WHAT ABOUT ME?) sit next to each other on a hard green sofa in a rented apartment. I see them sitting stiffly and apart, surreptitiously glancing, dissecting the other. Rose tells Sofia she is dying. It is only then that Sofia lets her head fall on to her mother's shoulder – a reach back – a touching without entanglement.'[7]

As Ava drops my hand and turns back to the TV I smile and tell her my hands used to look like hers and have springy, plump skin like hers, but I don't think she believes me.

≈

Like Lorde, Plath and Walker, I don't believe a woman must choose between fulfilment on the one hand or motherhood on the other. But it takes effort to summon the guts needed to go against the grain – if you don't want to choose between this or that, if you want to grab what is being offered in both hands. The self and the other, even if entangled, even if fully aware of the responsibility of care to the other, thrive better when the space between the two is honoured. Think of a

---

7 Deborah Levy, *Hot Milk* (London: Penguin Books), 2017.

fungal network which transports nutrients from the soil to the trees, and the trees send it carbon in return. They don't contaminate or suffocate the other; they sustain each other and grow.

I have a fantasy scene in mind when I think about the day Ava leaves home for the last time. I dream that I will feel nothing but happiness as I wave her goodbye, that she will close the door gently behind her and not slam it in my face. I then embark on the next stage of my own life, able to dedicate myself to founding my own existence in all three tenses again. I will never gaze at my hands and wish to be young again or feel queasy in the face of my daughter's youth. We will always be free to shape our own fates, yet we'll still be entangled enough to want to return freely to each other's sides from time to time – to glance at each other's hands in gentle conversation, to observe each other's shifting lifelines.

In my dream the push-pull is over.

SHAME 'N' SCANDAL IN THE FAMILY

Otherwise known as Aunty Mel's Baby

An Extract

Joyanna Lovelock

Aunty Mel had no idea how she'd become pregnant. How could she be, she asked me one Saturday night, right in the middle *of Life in Hopeful Village* (my favourite radio drama), as if a nine-year-old would know, when she had only done it the once? I couldn't help her there, as my Discovering Science classes hadn't stretched that far. As far as she could make out, she was quick to tell me, things did not happen quite so fast in the *True Confessions* she read, which she wasn't really supposed to, being a good Christian girl and that. The girls in those stories usually had a few goes at *it* before they 'got caught', and it was pages into the story before they missed their monthlies and went bawling to their boyfriends.

The most Aunty Mel remembered of what she called that *awful night* was a lot of fumbling and rumbling in the dark on the back seat of the rascal's old Zephyr in a disused warehouse car park. Besides, she was barely seventeen and only a few weeks into her first real job at Wei Chong's travel service in the bustling Parade Square of downtown Kingston, where she filed invoices and ran errands. And so far she'd had only one pay packet, so this couldn't be happening. But the endless trips to the wooden-surround latrine at the back of the house in the early hours of the mornings and a craving for jam and onion sandwiches could not be denied: Melvita Rhattigan was having a baby. *The dolly-house mash-up.*[8]

The question that loomed large was how to tell her God-fearing mother, my sweet Granny Dee. She feared Granny Dee would be destroyed by this manifest display of that dastardly sin of fornication. And quite rightly so. To have her hitherto untainted and untouched girl-child, her 'baby', pregnant and without a ring on her finger – because, according to Granny Dee, that was the only way any girl (well, any decent one) should ever conceive – that would be too much for her to bear. This, she assumed, would have devastating consequences on Granny's standing as a deaconess, third-in-charge and Head of Flowers and their Arrangements at the Redeemed at Last Gospel Tabernacle situated at the junction of Hagley Park Road and Old Hope Road. As a pillar of the community and a leading light of the congregation, Granny Dee had a responsibility to keep her household in check. That is, unmarried girls should not be going around getting pregnant.

Now, as is customary in these circumstances, Granny Dee would be summoned before the governing body, the Church Board, to explain herself. She could expect no mercy from

---

8 A Jamaican saying meaning plans have gone awry.

the Reverend Jeremiah Hazard, the new senior pastor, who left compassion on the doorstep when he arrived from the country parish of Fallon Gully. Word reached him that Sister Delores's daughter, Oralee, was a regular at Smokey Joe's all-night shebeen[9] over at Deanery Park. This den of iniquity, as he liked to call the place, formed the staple of his weekly rebukes – by that I mean his style of sermons. The very mention of the word 'shebeen' would fire up the congregation till the Holy Ghost licked them, whereby a sister or a brother or several of them would cry out, 'Have Mercy, yes, Lawd Jesus' or, 'Preach it, brother, preach it', washed down by a hearty dose of, 'Haaae...men! Haaae...men!'

***

Considering her daughter's somewhat immoral proclivities, Sister Delores was promptly relieved of her post as choir leader, a position she had held since time began. Under threat of withholding her substantial tithes and offerings – substantial because she was a rich and fulsome widow who had inherited half a fortune from her late husband Brother Orris (the other half went to his long-term mistress and her three sons) – she was reinstated with equal speed. My Granny Dee was not the militant type. Neither did she have any money to use as a weapon.

Better was expected of her, Aunty Mel reasoned to herself. She was no dance-hall party-hearty hussy. She was the last of Granny's ten children and, unlike the others, she wanted for nothing. Only the best for our Aunty Mel. She was one of a handful of people in the local area who

---

9 An illicit party.

ate breakfast cereal at breakfast time. Others settled for a wedge of hard-dough bread and a mug of cocoa tea. And the less well-off had to make do with some bush tea.[10] She was the only one of Granny's brood to be privately educated at the elite and expensive church school on the corner of South and Milton streets, where a girl was expected to nab a reverend-parson-in-the-making, as well as collect a few pieces of paper[11] if she had time.

She had piano lessons for a while from Mother Gentry, who ran a little private school for three to six-year-olds at her place down the hill, which I attended until I went to primary school. Despite all the money spent on it, Aunty Mel never got to grips with the treble clef and could seldom find her middle C, so that was abandoned in due season, much to her mother's regret. Nonetheless, Aunty Mel tried needlecraft, for which she did not possess any natural aptitude but, against all odds, she produced a beautiful crochet creation in pure and dazzling white, which was proudly displayed on the centre table in the parlour. Poor Granny Dee never missed an opportunity to draw it to the attention of anyone who so much as passed by the gate. Aunty Mel could carry a tune, though, and Grandpa always said she had a good sing. Music lessons and needlecraft classes did not come free or cheap, especially when money was thin on the ground. Grandpa hardly had any earnings to speak of from his infrequent carpentry stints with his cousin Jules, who held the belief that as family one should not expect to be paid for one's labour. And so, many times Grandpa was broke. Flat. Broke.

---

10 Hot herbal drinks made from branches and twigs.

11 College certificates.

Granny Dee acquired most of the money for Aunty Mel's extracurricular activities by washing and ironing for the great and the good, which involved the heavy khaki uniform of half of Jamaica's Defence Force. Pure torture for Granny Dee, doing other people's laundry for meagre wages and with not even so much as a 'Tank you and galang'.[12] Whilst she was quite happy to take care of her own family's household needs, it cut her to the quick that she had to resort to doing other people's dirty clothes. She considered herself a woman of noble birth who, as a girl, was happily ensconced in a big house in the coastal town of Savanna-la-Mar (commonly known as Sav-la-Mar) in the parish of Westmorland, with a retinue of servants in tow and a personal maid of her own.

Her father, son of a British slave owner, was at one time a wealthy farm owner; a man blessed with striking good looks but not the good sense to go with it. Aged forty-six, he lost his life too soon because he could neither hold his drink nor his tongue. After a mysterious disappearance of three months his mangled body was washed up at the mouth of Sherman's River in the neighbouring district of Moriah Bay. His untimely death left the family (wife and five offspring) with huge debts, which could only be resolved by a repossession of the land, which ultimately placed them in reduced circumstances. When Grandpa, a local handyman who did odd jobs around the farm and a master carpenter in training, and who did not have two (spare) farthings to rub together, came a-calling and in due season asked for Granny Dee's hand, she could hardly refuse. At least he had a trade. They would have a roof over their heads, and he would not allow his family to starve. For sure. Be that as it may, Grandpa

---

12 'Thank you and goodbye.'

was not readily accepted into Granny Dee's family. Him too dark, they said. Not that it bothered her. She had always been happy with her 'African Prince Maas Benji', and did not care who was enamoured or objected. For most of their union, Granny Dee stayed home and raised the children, and it wasn't until Aunty Mel started at the high school that Granny took up outside work. Aunty Mel had, in short, a lot to be thankful for.

* * *

The unspoken question was whether Granny Dee would throw her out to fend for herself in a hitherto unknown world in her single and pregnant state, in an attempt to lessen the sting of shame and scandal she would undoubtedly face from her sanctimonious church brethren and equally straitlaced neighbours. Or would she just kill her?

Aunty Mel spent more time than she should have pondering these thoughts. More than she should have. Better to blurt it out. When she did decide to tell Granny Dee, I, anticipating a nasty scene, made myself scarce by engaging in meaningless conversation with next-door's dog, Samson. I do not know how Aunty Mel told her mother she was pregnant. Anyhow, when she did tell her, Granny Dee was not to be found in the kitchen stirring her sweet-potato pudding, as was her wont on a Thursday afternoon after she had done her ironing. Her response was not what Aunty Mel expected. Granny Dee was sitting in the shade under the pomegranate tree fanning flies and other insects with her wide-brimmed straw hat. Her mood was muted. She listened in apparent silence, head presumably bowed in shame, and said nothing. Not a word. The absence of the expected shouting, wailing and gnashing of teeth unnerved me. *Did she really kill her?* I wondered.

Not a woman to be easily tempted by the Devil (Grandpa had told me that is where all temptations come from), Granny Dee remained true to the seventh commandment and Aunty Mel lived. What exchanges passed between mother and daughter on that occasion I never knew, and still don't to this day. But from all accounts it appeared that Granny took the view that 'these things are sent to try us'. She was that kind of a woman. *'tan' up* in the face of adversity. She was obviously disappointed in this state of affairs, but it was a disappointment she would bear with dignity. Yet it still begged the question: what to do with her?

***

Things were definitely on the change. For me. No more me and Aunty Mel sneaking off to the Carib Theatre at Cross Roads to catch a picture show. This egg-shaped structure with walls and ceiling designed to make you feel like you are under the Caribbean Sea, looking up at the surface, was a place of enchantment. I think about the times she took me to the National Stadium at the far, far end of Mountain View Avenue to see American singing stars like Pattie la Belle and the Bluebelles performing one of my favourite songs 'Down the Aisle I'll Walk with You', or Charles and Inez Foxx belting out their big song 'Mock-in', Bird, Yeah', and what a joy to see the new local singing sensation that was Millie Small. And she really was small. For true.

***

As the months drew on, Aunty Mel began to show, and everybody who lived on the hill knew that she was 'with child'. Whilst they might have felt that that was a very unhappy predicament for a young girl to find herself in, the situation was made worse when there was no clear-cut contender as to the identity of the baby's father. There was nobody to finger in that regard. Aunty Mel was never seen with a boy, walking with a boy, holding hands with a boy. No. As far as anyone could tell she'd never had a boyfriend. And there was no obvious reason for that. She was not bad looking. She could even be a pretty girl, but was never allowed to make much of herself. She had a shapely and well-defined body, which she hid most of the time under a shapeless shift dress. Vanity was not encouraged in Granny Dee's household. No sah! Aunty Mel was only allowed a little face powder on top of her Pond's cold cream, like her mother. And that was only for church. She had good hair, but fancy hairstyles were out, and she wore it scraped back in a ponytail. All the time. But she displayed a shyness which on a good day made her cute.

These traits were lost on the local boys, however, who found her snooty and aloof, and not without reason. When they tried to chat her up or ask her for a date, she would throw them a look that asked, *Who, me?* The boys in the church were goodly and godly enough, but even so, some would have liked to get to know her in the… biblical sense. You know, like, 'Adam knew Eve, his wife and she conceived and bore Cain.' Aunty Mel used to tell me that she would not let the boys feel her up for nothing, not like her slack friends Olga and Peggy, who had all the boys on the hill feeling them up all the time. I told her that I would let Byron Fernandes feel me up for a bag of paradise plums and she boxed me. I don't think she really meant to, but her hand had left her side and found my face before she could stop herself. After that I kept 'feel up' and Byron Fernandes to myself. So it was not surprising that those who knew of this imminent arrival were convinced they were witnessing an immaculate conception on an ecclesiastical level and an updated version of the Virgin Birth. Nineteen-sixties style!

* * *

Then Fonzo shows up! The baby father. Six months after the event. That is, the inception. It was a bright sunshine Sunday afternoon and I had returned from Trailblazers, the young people's arm of the church, where I learnt the Morse code, and how to salute my elders and march in a straight line in my starched khaki skirt and blouse. There he was, black as night, with his two gold teeth in the wrong place, in Granny Dee's parlour, perched on her high seat (usually reserved for the reverend pastor when he dropped by). Brazen as you please. Granny Dee and Grandpa were so excited to see him that they called the neighbours to come see. Shortly after Fonzo's arrival, these neighbours were bringing round fry plantain, rice and peas, escovitch[13] fish, curry ram goat, bammy,[14] fresh fruits like June plum and naseberry and gizzada[15] for him, the gentleman (as they called him). A feast. One helluva feast! Me tell you! One man even turned up with some Strong Back Soup (a mixture of Irish moss, Dragon Stout, Guinness, ginger, nutmeg, vanilla, condensed milk and some Wray & Nephew rum). Some of the above or all of them. No matter. Said to have medicinal properties like

---

13 Seasoned Red Snapper fried in oil to make the skin crispy, topped with onions and bell pepper.

14 Cassava flatbread.

15 The Jamaican brownie.

the soon-to-be-discovered Viagra! What he needed that for now was beyond me.

What Granny Dee and Grandpa talked about with Fonzo, I have no idea. When big people talking, I was not allowed in the room but sometimes I would kotch[16] behind the chicken coop and see if I could hear anything. I did not hear a thing of any significance as I recall, and certainly did not hear the 'married' word mentioned. I was quite disappointed. I like a good wedding. My Uncle Lloyd's wedding five years earlier was magical. All candles and darkness. Church. Catholic.

***

The family's hope of moving up the social and religious ladder rested heavily on Aunty Mel. She was expected to marry a minister of the gospel, or at the very least the son of one, in the hope that he would grow into one. That's the reason for Granny Dee's sacrifices. The reasons why she was prepared to wash and iron other people's rough clothes, so that Aunty Mel would be moulded and shaped into parson's wife material. Sending her to the church school was a start where she was bound to be acquainted with a few prospectives. But Fonzo, with his beat-up Zephyr and nicotine-stained fingertips was certainly no son of a preacher man. It was the first time I had clapped eyes on Fonzo. And the last. Aunty Mel didn't see too much of him after that either…

To be continued

---

16 Hanging around.

FICTION

REBORN

Kate Blincoe

Only time I use my voice each day. Sometimes, anyway. Hmmm. Hmmm. Clear it. Make it bright and fresh. Hi guys! Morning! Hiya! Hiya! Jump around a bit. Shake my arms and hands. Energy, energy.

Put my make-up on. Perfect base. Lots of eye. Get the baby. Outfits, nappy, wipes, set up tripod, turn on lighting. Test shot. OK. 10 a.m. and we're going live.

Good. Went well. Back to bed now. Could eat. Could eat something. No food at all. One old bit of bread is all. Order something. Not now. Later. Don't want to look at likes. Later. See if it went well. It was fine. Sleep now. Thick and dark. Air like hot custard. Just want to lie here.

Slept for an hour. As night was bad. Might go out now. I won't. Will I?

Could eat?

Order a cheeseburger and fries. A hot smell like sick. Just Eat. I can't. Throw them in bin.

Drink a shot. Just to, you know. Feel more OK. Burns down my throat. Hits my stomach like fire. Softens my brow, kind of numbs my face. One more. Take my meds.

Eat some cold fries out of the bin. Disgusting. Why? You're meant to put washing-up liquid on them to stop that. I don't have any. The baby is staring at me. Eyes so glassy. Watching me as I slump there on the kitchen floor. I wipe my greasy fingers down the side of the bin. Long slug trails. 'Hey Elsie, Elsie. You OK, baby girl?'

I'll tell them tomorrow. About her.

Parcels arrive. Four. I cut them open. Expensive baby clothes in one. A new make-up launch. Lovely toys. Must write them down, #gifted, so I can share. Too many boxes in here. Hit 96k subscribers.

A bunch of flowers. 'From your top fan.' Red gold tulips. Pretty. I want to open one up. Climb inside. I put them in the sink.

A direct message on Insta; 'I want to fuck you till your dead.'

It's hot and stuffy today. Summer-holiday weather. I have to keep the blinds closed.

Hold the baby and watch YouTube then sleep.

***

Hit 100k overnight. My US and Australian followers. Immense. So happy. So tired.

Now I'll tell them. Put my make-up on, waterproof mascara. Drink a shot. Two. Three. Going live. Tragic news, guys. So devastated. Baby Elsie's blind. She will never see. From birth. Just been confirmed by the doctors.

I cried a bit. Just prettily. The numbers blow up. The comments. People are mad for it.

I need some food. Actually hungry today. Need to go out. But can't go right now. Maybe later. Order some sushi. Eat it all. Insane.

There's backlash too. I was ready for it. But my numbers are going up up up. 111k. I laugh and dance around the room. Record a short thank-you. Show a few #gifted items. One wants future collab. Might earn a bit more.

2 p.m. is a bad time. Pretend it's not happening. Awful. Scrunch up the letter on the fridge. 'Court summons. Must attend.' Watch TikTok. Will feel better when it's all over. Was meant to put on some nice clothes and go and be sorry. But I can't. For petty theft. Nothing bad. Nothing much. Just little things to make me feel better. I've been caught too many times. I don't go in shops now. I don't go in people's houses. I don't risk anything.

Realise I've not taken meds. Have two to make up for it. Take a shower. Cold water. It needs fixing.

Plan tomorrow's content. Want back to basics. Baby routine. Maybe weaning chat? She's so pretty.

No dinner. Had all that sushi. You get a lot of hate if you're not tiny. I don't really get hungry anyway.

So many messages from friends to reply to. Not my real friends. I don't have them any more. But these guys do care about me. Tell me I'm too thin. Tell me Elsie is beautiful.

Some people tell me I'm so ugly. Tell me I'm a freak. Tell me to get a life. Tell me to take my clothes off.

Hardly sleep all night. Take a pill to help. It's bright so early. Sun streams through my crappy blinds. Crash in early hours. Oversleep for my live. Fuck. Everyone is going wild. 'Is she OK?'

Get on at 12 and explain that I took Elsie to the doctor's as she had a fever. Nice live with lots of practical content about caring for a poorly baby.

Sleep on sofa. Sweaty, clammy air. Woken by a thud on balcony door. Weird.

Open balcony door and hear the city below. So much noise. It makes my heart fizz and pop. A siren. A horn blaring. Ugh. Too much. The sun is shining intensely and it's hot. Should leave the door open but I don't like the noise. Bright light's not good for filming. Feel the sun on my skin for a moment. Close my eyes. What was that thud, though?

There. On the floor of the balcony, next to barren plant pot. A small, crumpled body. I bend down. A slick of the darkest midnight-blue feathers. I touch it. Warm. Turn it. A white chest and red splash of its throat. Not blood. The tiniest scarlet feathers. I gasp at its beauty. Its head flops. It's dead. Its wing is funny, twisted. Broken. This bird will never fly again. I pick it up gently in my hands – it hardly weighs a thing – and suddenly I'm crying. Crying hard for the bird, and for me.

Letting my howl ring out over this broken city, tears spill down my face and on to the feathers.

It twitches in my hands. I flinch and freeze. Hold it so gently. Its eyes are open. Looking at me. It's alive.

'Oh!' I exclaim out loud.

I stand there for five minutes, wondering what to do, staring at every detail of this creature. Little curled brown toes, like wire. Elegant, long forked tail tickling my arm. The pool of black around the pool of each eye. Time stands still.

I bring it inside and tip new shoes I will never wear out of their box, placing it inside on one of Elsie's nappies. It lies there. One wing out funny. Watching me.

I Google what it is, and what to do. It's a swallow. It came here from Africa. All the way from Africa and I can't even leave my flat. Says it has no chance of survival. Some birds you can help, but not swallows. I will have to watch it die, and I can't bear that.

It hit my window. It's my fault. I will make it better. I put a pointless dish of water in the shoebox, and it shuffles away. Elsie stares blankly. She looks dumb now. Inert.

I pick Elsie up; her solid little weight is a comfort. I tell her what the bird is and where it came from. Her head lolls. I do love her, I really do. But I feel so stupid too. I never meant for this to happen. Maybe it's why I hide away, like she is my captor – because I'm embarrassed. And the world is so cruel too.

I've always loved dolls. Most people outgrew them, but I never did. I liked caring for something, even when I couldn't care for myself.

When I pose Elsie and hold my hand just so behind her head, making little motions, she looks so alive. Everyone says she is beautiful and hyperreal. She was hand-painted by an amazing artist, and I paid over £500 for her, but that's not it. I am very good at what I do – the styling, the chat, how I hold her – and that makes the difference in people caring about her. I was voted one of the top ten reborn channels on YouTube last month.

I wrap her in a blanket, covering her face. Feeling disloyal. She is my world, but right now I need to think without her constant blank gaze. It means I can open the blinds, too, without risking the sunlight damaging her silicone. I need to know what to do with this little broken creature that has flown into my life.

I find out the bird eats insects. I'd hoped I could get some fruit or seeds for it, but that's not what it needs. My pillow calls to me in that magnetic way, like I can no longer be upright. But the bird looks at me intensely. Its shiny black eye focused on me, watching me when I move.

'OK, OK!' I say out loud. 'I'll get you something.'

My pulse quickens as I put on some trainers. They feel tight and too restrictive. I take them off and grab some flip-flops. I step out of my flat, not sure at all what my plan is. The corridor swims around me. Grey walls closing in, the floor swaying under me, I collapse to my knees. It stinks of cannabis. I get up and carry on. A thudding in my ears make me see strange flashes of light and colour. A scream is rising up in my throat. It might come out. It's like I'm already screaming. Perhaps I am. But I look down at my feet – flip-flop – and they keep moving. Down the stairs – can't take the lift. Three flights. And I open the door, hit by a wall of heat and the smell of a summer's day in the city. The tarmac is melting, the petrol fumes are high. Cut grass somewhere. Sun cream.

It was cold last time I was outside. There was ice on the trees and it looked so pretty.

I make my way to the park just across the way. It's my only idea.

Other birds just like mine are in the air. Swooping, and making sharp turns that make my heart soar. Forked tails like streamers. Like holiday. I can't take my eyes off them. I must make my swallow better. I must help my bird soar again.

The sun is hot on my skin. Shines like liquid gold. I will burn soon. Elsie's silicone would go soft with these intense rays. Her pretty pink lips would fade. The grass in the park has been cut; it's bright green and sticks to my toes. It smells like childhood. Like playing outside with my brother. Melting ice creams and inflatable beachballs sticky with our fingers.

I don't know how to do this.

A thickset man wearing gym gear walks by and stares at me. 'All right, sweetheart? You OK there, darlin'?' I'm sitting by the pond trying to work out what to do. I don't know if he is hitting on me, just being friendly or concerned about my well-being. I stare back blankly, trying to read his meaning. 'Might never happen, love,' he says. 'Cheer up!' And he walks away, whistling.

I don't know how to do this.

A fly buzzes past. I make a half-hearted grab at it. Impossible.

The pond is green and murky. It's only half full. Cracked, dried mud surrounds the edge where the water level has dropped. The stagnant whiff of rotting fishy vegetables reaches my nostrils. I gag and start to get up.

But there at the side is a little pocket of water. A mini pond. Floating on the top of it are insects. Most dead, some wiggling and struggling to escape. Before I can think, I scoop my hands into the revolting gunk and capture as many creatures as I can. I run across the park, hands cupped in front of me, gruesome pond juice dripping down my arms. I think of the bird and grip my fingers together tightly.

I have to ask a woman to help me open the main door. She looks at me with wide, startled eyes but does what I ask. 'Thank you!' I shout, running through. My voice rings out loudly into the air. So unfamiliar. I take the stairs two at a time, my breath coming fast and sharp in my chest. At my flat, I have to use my key and spill the last drops of pond. But the little bugs remain, stuck to my hand. I'm in.

The swallow is laying on its side. Could it have died? I turn it gently and the blackberry eye looks at me. Alert. I take a still-wiggling gnat off my hand and, with my eyebrow tweezers, place it carefully in the bird's slightly open beak. It pauses a moment, frozen, then as if it's worked out what's happening, moves its head in a little shake and eats the insect. Then opens its beak for more. A giggle is rising in my throat. I push it down to continue my job, hands as steady as they can be. Heart still pounding from the stairs, blood pulsing in my arms. We keep going, for about twenty insects. Then I drip a little water into the beak.

The swallow rights itself, up to standing. That wing still held out to the side.

Elounda. A white taverna next to the turquoise sea. A girl in a pretty sundress. A mother, a father, a brother. Sitting by the shore, eating calamari and Greek salad. Birds like this flitting high and low, swooping for insects, visiting again and again their nests in the eaves where gaping mouthed chicks squeak for more food. Sun on my skin. Before it all went wrong. Elounda.

I lay on the sofa and sleep. Thick and dark. Like wading through treacle. In my nose, in my eyes, in my lungs.

It's night when I wake. Just after 11 p.m. Elounda is making a noise, a scruffling. He's probably hungry. I can't go outside to get more insects. I stand and stretch, swimming through a wave of nausea. I've not eaten all day. I'm going to have to go out for him.

I turn on the light. Elounda is up on his little legs and turns his head to me. I take a shot of vodka to galvanise me. Nothing galvanises like vodka. And this time I grab a mug to hold the insects.

It's no good. The room is spinning. Dark closing in from the sides of my eyes. I lie on the floor. My heart is throbbing through my entire body like it might burst out through my face.

He's scruffling.

I breathe.

And sit. Head between my knees. Maybe I need to eat something.

I crawl to the cupboard, seeing how dirty my lino is, and pull out a box of old cereal. I plunge my hand in and shove Cheerios into my mouth. They are soggy. A cardboard mulch. But the sweetness is like a buzz through my body. I eat more and more – out of my hand, like it's a trough, dropping them all around me. A scattering of little rings. A sigh eases out of me, like I've been holding my breath for too long.

I can stand. Carefully I pick up the mug.

'I'll be back soon,' I tell Elounda. I pick up my phone, and it is heavy with notifications. I put it down again. 'Back soon, my boy.'

Going out is easier in the dark. People don't look at you so much. There aren't so many cars. I'm into the park before I can stop to think. It's not safe in here at night, not for women, everyone knows that. I hold the key poking through my clenched fist. Weaponised. I keep my head down.

I get to the pond and kneel. I know what to do now. Skim the top of the water with my mug, by the shallow edge. Insect soup for Elounda. And my heart is racing and I'm getting back. I'm back in the door and I'm into my flat and he's waiting for me and he's hungry. Silken gloss, blue-black shine. Blackberry eye. His perfection so intense it aches my chest. I pick up his feather-weight, careful of his wing, and sit him on the table. On my finger, dip for little insects stuck. Tweezers. Gaping beak. We know what to do now.

Then I clean out his box – fresh bedding and water. Pop him back in.

Read some more about him. Mealworms might be good. Might help him get his strength up. His friends will be leaving in a few weeks, back to Africa. Will he join them? Will he die in here in my shoebox? He can't survive the winter here.

Everyone's worried about Elsie. I have more than 300 direct messages and at least 500 comments. It's too much. I can't reply to them all.

I'll have to do a live. A normal, boring live. Tomorrow morning. 10 a.m. I set an alarm. I'll need time to get insects before. I go to bed.

***

I don't sleep well, but that's my own fault for sleeping so much in the day. Still, I'm up and it's bright and I'm dressed in a pretty sundress for the live and I get insects and I stop in at the corner shop and buy some food for me too. Some bread and butter and jam and milk and apples.

I order mealworms online, special delivery. They look gross. They will come today, still alive.

I put Elounda in my bedroom for the live. In case he makes a noise. He's moving more today.

I unwrap Elsie, and I'm sorry that she has been left ignored. We do a nice, simple live. All about keeping baby cool in the hot weather, water-play and sun hats. It's cute and I'm able to show a few little summer outfits that have arrived recently, and a sun suit that is adorable. I don't even address the comments that say I'm having some sort of a crisis. I just get on with being bright and chatty and doing what I do best.

I eat an apple. It's amazing. Then two bits of toast with jam and butter.

A delivery. More heatwave clothes for Elsie, probably. But the usual guy hands me a small parcel, carefully wrapped. Fragile.

I open it slowly, and prise off the lid of the small tin. A wriggling mass of maggoty worms. They smell sweet, like chicken. I turn and gag. But bring myself back. I can't believe I'm doing this. They are an insane source of protein for Elounda. I take my tweezers and gently pick one out. It writhes and I'm scared I'll squeeze it too hard. I pop it in Elounda's shoebox, and he eyes it. What am I going to do with them if he doesn't like it?

Then he drops his head and pecks it up. I want to whoop!

He eats seven. I hold him to my chest, just to soak up his beauty, and he grips on to my top with his little claws. I sit on the sofa with him there and close my eyes. He climbs up into my hair and nestles there, resting with me. I put him back when he gets fidgety. To make sure he didn't get all tangled up.

I don't have to go out. I have food for Elounda, and for me. But I do. I go to the park and sit for ten minutes on the grass. Without my phone. Just watching. The caress of the sun on my skin, eyes closed for a few minutes. The world moving around me.

Back in the flat it's stuffy and Elounda is restless. He's moving lots. His wing is much less crooked. I open a window and a breeze tickles into the room. Why did I worry so much about letting outside air in?

I reply to some messages and talk to a promoter. They want me to do an interview with a magazine. About the rebirth of the reborn or some such. I'm not sure. I normally say no to that stuff, but I might do it. There's a photo shoot. I'd love to do that, but I look such a wreck. It's not for a month. Maybe with some more time outdoors I'd get a bit more colour. Maybe if I eat and sleep a bit better?

Elounda stretches both his wings to their full length. If one had been broken, surely he wouldn't be able to do that yet? His feathers shine in the sunlight. Iridescent beetle back. Miracle of nature on my coffee table.

'I love you,' I say out loud. Shocked by the truth. Shocked that I feel anything at all, let alone such a deep pure emotion as I do for this fragile creature. But I think I might be saying it for myself too. Just a little.

A heavy lumbering bluebottle flies in through my window, buzzing laboriously, bumping on to the mirror. Like a flash of lightening, like a streak of magic, Elounda is in the air. He catches the fly and circles, a lap of glory, of fluid control, of aerial beauty. And he is gone, out of my window, flash of forked tail and gone.

Tears stream down my face. I'm on my knees. It's happy, though. I mended him. I saved him.

'I'll come. I'll come and visit you in Africa,' I say into the air, into the void he has left. I can't think of anything better. It will be my goal. To get myself well enough, to sort some stuff out. Then I'll go to the place he came from, to the place he will return.

BURGUNDY SATIN
MANOLO BLAHNIK PUMPS
– SIZE 6

Emma Gow

The shoes sat there in their virtual online basket – alone but defiantly still in stock – for weeks before I finally mustered the courage to press *complete order*. Afterwards, I closed the browser page and slammed the lid of my laptop shut, scarcely able to believe I'd actually gone and done it.

Two days earlier, having had a very good day at work and with the word *bonus* ringing cheerfully in my ears, I made the incredibly foolish mistake of showing Mother the shoes on my phone, naïvely hoping she would share my enthusiasm and perhaps encourage me to spend a little of my hard-earned money on myself for once.

'You can't wear those,' she said. 'Girls like you are different, Stella.'

'Girls like me?' I asked.

'Aye. Steady. Dependable. Men of good stock don't marry girls that look flashy or showy. You're a nice girl. People expect you to dress a certain way.' She sniffed, her face scrunching in disapproval. 'They don't wear those,' she said, and waved the photo away. I slipped my phone back into my pocket, shame burning my cheeks.

Where had being that sort of girl got me, though? That question had sprung unbidden into my head more frequently of late. Being the person my mother required me to be seemed to mean no one actually wanted to marry me. I wasn't proud to admit that my brown faux-leather court shoes with their one-inch heels and sensible polycotton work suits in a variety of comfortably sludgy tones weren't exactly luring sailors to a watery fate. I didn't even want to get married, not really. I wasn't even sure if I liked men – I certainly hadn't liked any of the ones I had encountered so far, anyway.

'They aren't exactly banging down the door for me just now, Mum, all these wonderfully bred men out there who are so set on marrying,' I snapped later, attempting to scrub the many-ringed tea stains out of Mother's cups at the kitchen sink, a thankless task at the best of times made infinitely worse by her judgemental commentary. My status as an old maid had been reinforced by the announcement of the betrothal of yet another faceless daughter of one of her friends to a spongy-faced accountant who looked like he probably smelled of ham. The shoes had served to add one more level of cement to its foundations. The cups had reached the stage that the stains were probably holding them together – you'd have more chance of cleaning Lady Macbeth's hands. But Mum refused to get new ones. 'Soak them in Milton and run a brillo round them and they'll be beautiful,' she insisted. They never were. They just stank. Still, I kept trying to restore them to their former glory.

'That's because you're too choosy,' she answered, perched no more than ten inches away from the TV. The light from the screen cast ghastly blue-green shadows on her already too-pale skin, while her red hair – piled high on top of her head and fixed in place with approximately half a can of Elnett firm-hold hairspray – glowed almost ethereally, an Irn-Bru-hued halo. The volume on the TV was turned right up to thirty-eight, which seemed to me to be the perfect level for inflicting acute psychological distress. I had heard the telly from the street outside as I walked up the path and had briefly paused, keys in hand, wondering if I had the strength to endure an hour of *Tipping Point* at full volume before I could escape to prepare dinner. Maybe I could go to the station and get on the next train to somewhere. Anywhere. As usual, my sense of duty won out and I trudged my way into the house.

'You even turned down that nice Dave – now that could have been the making of you, a fella with a steady job like that. He wouldn't want you in those shoes, though!' she scoffed. Tendrils of smoke from her cigarette trailed a lazy path to the ceiling, deepening the mustard-yellow stain on the peeling Anaglypta wallpaper.

I knew there was no point arguing with her. Dave worked in the local post office and was nearly ten years my senior but looked significantly older in his cardigan – complete with leather elbow patches – and brown corduroy trousers. He spoke with a wheezing rasp and coughed for a full thirty seconds after each bout of laughter before depositing a hearty hock of phlegm into one of the many handkerchiefs stashed around his person in between his dubious attempts at flirtation.

'Stella?' he'd say. 'Like the lager? I hope you aren't as expensive! Ha ha ha.' Cough splutter snort repeat.

It was not meant to be.

My achievements never seemed to matter to Mother – that I had a 'steady job' of my own which probably paid twice more than those held by the hapless individuals she foisted on to me was neither here nor there. It wasn't much, but I'd got my very own little flat and mortgage, and had just paid off the last of my student loans the month before. I was slowly learning Portuguese on an app during my daily walk to work. I could make a twice-baked soufflé that was a little pot of cheesy heaven, and I had even plumbed in my own toilet by following videos on the internet. The idea that having someone like Dave as a partner would enrich my life in any way was risible. So what if I was being choosy? I knew, deep down, that I was worth so much more, and was practically incandescent that no one else saw it.

I carried that anger with me for two days, a tiny red-hot ball of indignation whose strength never abated. Usually I'd brush off Mother's barbed words with a laugh and shake of the head, convincing myself they were said out of concern and not intended to hurt, but I couldn't do it any more.

I gave myself permission to feel it all – all the pain and rage at the sheer lack of recognition of what was right for me and all the snide, half-whispered jibes about being left on the shelf or possibly needing to buy a cat soon. Not. Any. More.

Earlier today, though, something shifted. As I sat in the office break room, absent-mindedly eating a Gregg's cheese and onion pasty and half-listening to Anne from reception talk about the upcoming end-of-quarter work night out, I felt my rage morph into something less spiky, less destructive. The quiet, usually ignored voice that whispered tales about great journeys I could take suddenly grew louder. The self-deprecation and humility that had been drummed into me year after year, all the instructions to stand straight and smile more and try and be more agreeable, for goodness' sake, began to diminish. I wasn't angry any more. I was energised.

At home, I opened the page on my laptop where the beautiful shoes lived and stared at them, resplendent in their perfect, shiny satin-covered glory. Suddenly all the reasons not to buy them – Mother's reasons, Society's reasons – didn't seem as compelling.

They will never make it out of the box. Sure they will. I'll put them in a stand in my hall so I can see them as soon as I walk through my front door. I'll take a photo of them and use it as the wallpaper on my phone so they'll pop up every time I get a message.

You've not got anywhere to wear them. I'll wear them in the kitchen when I'm baking. I'll wear them when I clean the bathroom. I'll wear them in my jammies while I'm watching *Strictly*. I'll wear them to all the weddings of strangers that you'll inevitably make me go to. I'll wear them to your funeral. I'll wear them to my own.

They aren't worth all that money. They are worth it to me. And I am worthy of having beautiful things, even if you don't think so.

People like you don't own things like that. Correction: people like me *didn't* own things like that. Until now. Just you wait and see.

ETERNAL NOW AND THE FRAILTY
OF HUMAN PERCEPTION

Jan Kaneen

Joan's sitting on the faded chintz sofa, arms crossed, plimsols jiggling, breathing in the exciting smell of pressure-cooked cabbage. Her unblinking gaze is fixed on Great Uncle Arnold as she breathes in, breathes out, breathes in, breathes out. Great Uncle Arnold's sitting opposite in his battered armchair – the one that's the colour of porridge and always feels scratchy when you brush past it. He reaches up to the rosewood tallboy to switch off the wireless that sits on top, and Joan's eyes move as he moves, taking in every twitch and flicker. When he puts a bangers-and-mash forefinger over his lips to make the special sign for keeping secrets, the excitement in the room thickens like gravy. In that new, thick quiet the grandmother clock standing stiff and upright in the alcove by the open fire seems to stop ticking, and Joan holds her breath.

Great Aunt Ada's gone outside – up the garden to peg out the clothes. Wonderful things never happen when Great Aunt Ada's indoors, and Joan's not even sure why she's called *great* Aunt Ada at all. Happen it's because she's married to Great Uncle Arnold. Married ladies take their husband's

95

surnames – Joan knows that, because her mam told her so – so happen they take their great names too, and it's plain as yesterday why Great Uncle Arnold's called *great* Uncle Arnold. But whatever the reason, ever since Great Aunt Ada went outside, Joan's been feeling like she did last Christmas, all fluttery and fizzy and can't-sit-still.

She'd felt the first flicker of it walking back after school dinners. Great Aunt Ada always collects her from school after dinners on a Monday because infants finish early – at one o'clock – and Joan's mam has to work lates cleaning the hospital till long gone teatime. Joan holds her great aunt's hand as they walk up Hunger Hill – past the newly built black-and-white semis that stand in the place the bombed-out terraces used to be. But today, when they turned into the small council estate where Great Aunt Ada's lived for donkey's years, Joan noticed the trees had all changed colour. The leaves had been green the week before, she was sure of that, but today they were yellowish gold, and when they caught the gusting wind they sounded like the waves had at Whitby when they'd crashed over the stone harbour, all noisy and exciting, on their rainy summertime daytrip.

Joan took it all in – the crispy wind, the seaside leaves, the Christmassy feeling inside her tummy, but to be absolutely sure, she squeezed her great aunt's hand and asked, 'Is it a good day for drying?

Great Aunt Ada's thin face had looked surprised but pleased to be asked.

'Aye, child,' she'd said, lifting her expert gaze to the shifting clouds. 'It's fine and fresh – a champion day for drying.'

Great Aunt Ada always does the laundry on Mondays – dolly-boards the clothes in the morning in the big white sink while Joan's at school, then puts them through the mangle to wring out the worst of the water. She does the pegging out once she and Joan are safely indoors. It takes her ages, because if there's one thing Great Aunt Ada can't stand it's messy pegging. The pegs have to be exactly the right distance apart, and the socks have to be hung in matching pairs, and apart from the socks, every peg has to join two bits of washing, so it runs together like the bunting did at the new queen's coronation in summer, looping between the streetlamps all the way down Hunger Hill.

When Joan heard those magic words, *a champion day for drying*, the flutter of excitement right in the middle of her was completely different from the rainy-day clench of disappointment the Monday before. *That* Monday, Great Aunt Ada had marched her home under the shadow of the big black brolly and they'd splashed up Hunger Hill all brisk and quick without saying a word. When they got indoors, Great Aunt Ada had set to work lowering the iron clothes rack from the kitchen ceiling, tutting and puffing with tight, thin lips and thunderstorm eyes, because if there's one thing makes Great Aunt Ada proper crotchety it's inside drying. It steams up the windows and the clothes don't get aired right and the whole house stinks of wet. By the time Great Aunt Ada had hauled the mangled clothes right up to the ceiling and wound the rope round the iron wall hook again and again in the shape of a sideways eight, the crossness had wafted right through the house, clean and cloying like Acdo soapflakes. The afternoon had lasted for ever as Great Aunt Ada tutted and dusted, jabbing at her plants and whatnots with short, sharp dabs as the rain lashed the back window. Great Uncle Arnold had stared at his newspaper, shaking the big grey pages straight when they needed turning so they made a crackly noise like his dodgy lungs. He'd hardly looked up at all, never mind made any secret signs, and Joan had sat quiet on the sofa looking at the pictures in her Noddy book as she breathed in the damp disappointment.

But not today. Today it's a champion day for drying and Great Aunt Ada's in the garden hanging out the clothes, and the pressure cooker's rattling and hissing in the kitchen next door, and there's only the thrilling whiff of gassy cabbage which they always have for Monday tea. Great Aunt Ada thinks Joan's too little to chew grown-up food, so they always have shepherd's pie with mashed carrots and swedes and soggy cabbage boiled till it's brown.

Great Uncle Arnold moves his pointy finger from his lips and curls it into a letter-C shape, then straightens it back up again, which is the sign that Joan should go over. She turns on to her tummy to wriggle off the sofa, and as she does she catches a glimpse of Great Aunt Ada through the back window struggling to peg out a big white shirt on to the line. The sleeves are flapping wildly in the wind, and a straggle of grey hair blows loose from her usually neat little bun. She looks even busier than usual. She'll be ages yet.

The flames in the fireplace dance amber as Joan moves towards her great uncle. His dark brown eyes spark with firelight as he leans down sideways to the bottom drawer of the tallboy. His silver hair doesn't move as he leans, but stays fixed in place, held by the special hair cream Great Aunt Ada buys for him in Timothy White's. He pulls the drawer open and takes out a tea tin with an enamelled picture of the new queen on top. Joan knows it's a tea tin because before the coronation, Great Aunt Ada threw a Littlewood's catalogue party in the posh front parlour. It was ladies only, so Great Uncle Arnold went down the Legion, and Joan did special helping, handing round the catalogues to all the old ladies then offering them the sugar bowl once their cups were full. They'd proper loved the coronation stuff, and ordered matching tins of tea and biscuits in preparation for the big day. But the tea's all used up now, and the tin's full of squares of something brown and shiny with swirly letters on top. Joan can't tell what the letters say, because she can't read properly yet, but they're pressed into the surface in curly handwriting, and she's sure the first letter is a *C.* She catches a faint whiff of something vaguely sweet and looks up into Uncle Arnold's firelight eyes. He says nowt as he picks up a square between his forefinger and thumb, then nods for her to do the same.

It doesn't feel squidgy like the midget gems he keeps in the middle drawer of his writing bureau, and it doesn't feel hard like the Murray Mints he hides in a white paper bag in the magazine rack. It's hard and melty at the same time, and Joan's warm fingers leave a lighter brown print on its surface. He pops it into his mouth in one quick movement and Joan copies him exactly.

It's nowt at first, and she's almost disappointed, but then it starts to melt, sweet and thick, mixing with her spit so she can hardly move her tongue. It's more delicious than anything she's ever tasted, warmer than dunked garibaldis, lovelier than Parma violets, sweeter than raspberry-ripple ice cream.

Time widens as the moment scorches itself into Joan's memory.

They'll do the same next week, and the week after that − a square of chocolate every Monday afternoon, so long as the weather stays fine, right up until Joan starts at big school and doesn't need picking up any more. Then the visits to her great aunt and uncle will become fewer and further between, what with hockey practice and homework and helping in the library, but Joan will never be too busy to regret the time she misses with Great Uncle Arnold. When Joan starts sixth form, Great Aunt Ada won't be able to do the washing by hand any more, on account of her arthritis, so Joan's mam will organise a machine on hire purchase, and Joan'll start coming round on Mondays again to do the unloading and pegging out. And when she does, Great Aunt Ada will nip down the Co-op because she doesn't like to leave Great Uncle Arnold on his own any more, what with his dodgy ticker and gas-damaged lungs, and Joan'll reinstate the chocolatey ritual with a bar she brings with her one day in her battered brown satchel. They'll keep it up almost every Monday until Joan becomes the first in her family to go to university. The day before she does, in September 1965, she'll visit her Great Uncle Arnold in Leeds General Infirmary. His breathing will be laboured and ragged after the heart attack, but when she offers him some chocolate instead of bringing grapes it'll rekindle the firelight in his cloudy eyes; then, just before the end of her first term, she'll come home a week early so as not to miss his funeral, and when the rest of the mourners sing 'Abide with Me' or 'Amazing Grace' (she'll never be able to remember which) she'll pop a square of chocolate onto the back of her tongue as tears prickle and stab behind her eyes. She'll have to press it hard into the roof of her mouth to stop herself dissolving into proper sobs. And five years later when she gets wed, she'll place saucers of chocolate on all the tables down the Legion, waiting till the end of Stevie's new-husband speech, when he makes the toast to absent friends before savouring a single square. And a year after that, when she has a child of her own, she'll cradle little Stephen Arnie in the crook of her left arm, daydreaming about how she'll replay the first-taste-of-chocolate moment once he gets old enough so the happiness will melt into him like it did into her. And for the thirty years she's a teacher then headmistress at the local primary school, she'll give gifts of chocolate to children who try hard, and it'll always make her smile when she sees the pleasure it brings. And when she's proper old and has forgotten almost everything else and has to move into sheltered accommodation for her own safety and her family's peace of mind, she'll chuck a chunk of chocolate into her mouth on fine, dry Mondays as her mind wanders wherever it will. And when, all over the country, the elderly and vulnerable are isolated to shield them from a virus that's wiping them out, when the exhausted carers inquire from behind their faceless masks if there's anything they can do to make her more comfortable, she'll mutter something about a wee taste of chocolate, because though she won't be able to remember why exactly, it'll still make her feel special right up to the end.

But back in the – let's call it 'moment', when Joan's hardly started to live her life, let alone watched the last remembered fragments of it flash back through her dying mind – both she and Great Uncle Arnold are oblivious to the infinity spooling through them like untold futures.

Great Uncle Arnold replaces the lid and returns the tin to the bottom drawer, taps the side of his nose with a Cumberland forefinger – the sign that it's all over for a week and Joan must keep the secret. The last tang of sweetness is fading from her tongue as she goes outside to help with the pegging. She skips through the long, dark ginnel that separates her great aunt and uncle's house from the one next door then hops down the concrete steps that lead to the lawn. A cold lick of wind catches her cheek – it feels nice and right and crisp and clean – so she lifts her chin to feel it deeper at the very same moment a bright-white shaft of lemonade light leaks through a crack in the billowing clouds.

FEATHERWEIGHT

Feline Charpentier

Her body weighed far more than he had expected, its heft catching him off balance, so that he stumbled as he tried to undo the tight cord. His wellies got stuck in the mud and straw of the cowshed, and he muttered and cursed, taking the full force of her limp body with his bad shoulder, trying to undo the knot in the woven baler twine with his free hand. Lewis had known it was too late, or so he said to me, later that afternoon, after the police had come and taken her away. He was still pale with the shock of it, as the words fell out of him.

He had come home as soon as they let him, and held my hand ever so gently. Did not spare any details – never mind I've not been to the cowshed in over twenty years. Lewis has never spared the details – he knows I live for the details. He'd known by the way she had hung so very still. A lead weight, as if a huge moth had cocooned itself, strung from silk, from the ancient oak beams running the length of the shed. Not spinning, or swaying, despite the north-westerly. Entirely still. As if in stasis, waiting for a new beginning.

'Such a waste, Siân,' he kept saying, shaking his head, stroking my hand, which still held in his. 'Such a terrible waste. She was such a pretty one. And her kids…'

I nodded, letting my hand be stroked, her children's faces in my head. Not that they were really children any more. Jan, he must be coming up to seventeen, maybe even eighteen by now. And Katrina, such a slight, timid girl, just becoming a young woman. Poor things.

I wondered where they were, who had told them – if it was Iwan, the nice young policeman, the one who came up to the farm sometimes to keep me up to date with news from town.

I hadn't seen her in nearly a year. They used to come all the time – her, the children, sometimes even her husband, the artist – bringing flowers, or biscuits, never announced, knowing I would always be in. She made jam with the damsons from our garden, and would bring the jars, gleaming and spiced with cinnamon, labels written in beautiful swirly script. Where she came from they ate it with black bread, and butter, a deep, golden yellow, she told me proudly. She couldn't make the bread here – the flour was never right.

They had been renting the cottage on the hill since the children were tiny. When Lewis had first come home and told me he had finally found tenants for the old place he said he couldn't say no. An artist, from London, his wife foreign, didn't speak much English. I had stopped going out by then – it was only a year or so after Cai. I was cross, thinking we'd have trouble. Hippies, foreigners. Wouldn't pay the rent; the lawn wouldn't get mowed.

A week later she came, calling out 'hullo' in her thick accent, coming straight up to the front door. I didn't let her in, of course – spoke to her out of the kitchen window. She didn't bat an eye, just kept smiling at me, her long blonde hair twirling in the wind as she spoke and waved her long arms at me, something about rain and mud and sky. She was thin as a rake; her legs looked as if they could hardly hold her upright. Stuck inside big old men's wellington boots, miles too big for her. Beautiful, but fragile, as if she was made of lace.

'Yes, it always rains here – you'll have to get used to it,' I had said, knowing how grumpy I sounded, not caring.

'Yes. Like home: lots of mud.' Her laugh, like a clear bell for church on Sundays, raucous and bigger than her, a small smile I couldn't help returning.

She came every week after that. Her English slowly improved. The children came with her. Jan – *Janosch* – was only a little boy then, not much older than Cai had been. It hurt to look at him. They came to the garden, and I would talk to them out of the window. They seemed to think that was normal, so when I asked them inside, one drizzling October day, they looked surprised. Katrina was only a baby then, strapped tight to her mother's chest, so that you could only see her little bald head, bobbing about. Jan came into our little kitchen, the fire crackling, the gas lamps sputtering, and he wandered about, touching everything. In his hands a fistful of small feathers. She saw me looking.

'He collects. All he can find, in the fields. Dirty, but I can't stop.' Shrugged her shoulders, smiled her church smile.

'Oh, it's OK, little boys, always collecting. Cai, he did the same.' Before I knew what I was doing, I had gone in the back and brought back the tiny glass bottle, the one I had put Cai's feathers in. Iridescent magpie tail feathers, the dun wing feathers of a sparrow, even swallow's down, tiny and gossamer soft. Little Jan had marvelled, and as he stroked them I told her everything, the words tumbling out.

I keep thinking about those oak beams. How Lewis's great-grandfather Idris could never have known what would one day come to pass in the shed he had built with his bare hands. His wrestling days long behind him, Idris had taken on his father's farm. Idris, the wrestler, Lewis's hero, came back when his leg refused to mend from a silly fall, when the crowds stopped wanting to see him win, and instead began to wince when he fell with a thud on the wooden floor of the ring. When he finally had to admit he would not again hear a cheer from the crowds of men around the ring.

Idris the fighter had come home and put all his anger into the land. With the money from his winnings he built the cowshed, got a small herd that grew to the hundred-strong Lewis still cusses over now. Giant, docile black-and-white ships that coast around the valley, chewing and pondering, making babies and milk and deepening Lewis's worry lines.

The cowshed was originally all oak frame, the sides mud and daub, the roof little chunks of slate hewn from the mine up the road. It's all corrugated now, rust-brown and rattling. But the oak frame remains, and even I remember the span of the beams – two-hundred-year-old giants, they must have been. With your hands splayed and spread out, thumbs touching, you would only just cover the width. You could still see the marks Idris's big chisels must have made. I imagine the weather-beaten hands of Lewis's grandfather smoothing over each stroke, the chipped hieroglyphics of his pattern, either end, where the A-frame slotted in. I think of all the thoughts he had while he toiled away, his disappointments and wishes all poured into this cowshed on a Welsh hill.

How could he have foreseen what that beam would one day help to do? Was it the fact of their heft that made her do it there? Is there a presence, some part of her haunting the space? Do the cows know? Lewis had to put them back in there, a week or so after the police had given him the all clear.

'Iwan says the family will come and see me – he thinks the artist'll want to move out.'

'Has he seen them? How are they?' Serving supper, a lamb hotpot, with beans from the freezer.

Lewis eats, his bald patch glowing in the dim lamp above the kitchen table. It makes him look almost holy, as if he were a visiting monk. I smile, cut him a slice of bread from the loaf sat beside his arm. Iwan, the policeman, knows everyone in town.

'He says they didn't say much, the kids. The girl, Katrina, poor slip of a thing, still just like her mother. He said she looked as if she hadn't slept.' He looks at me, continues. 'Siân, you're not to fret. There's nothing we can do.' Knows before I open my mouth what I'm going to say. 'And no, I'm not going up there – not yet. It's too soon. They'll think I want to talk rent. Give them time.'

I close my mouth again, shake my head, fold my hands into my lap. It's no use, I know he's probably right. Obviously I can't go, and if Lewis goes it won't look right.

'Can you at least leave something for them, at the gate? You can go late so they don't see you. Please.' I catch his eye, and he relents.

I gather them all up, run them through my hands to get the dust off and find the nicest little bottle in Cai's collection. The windowsill in Cai's bedroom, where all of his treasures live, is brightly lit in the afternoon sun. It glints and twinkles amongst the glass bottles and shells, the smoothest river pebbles and little wooden figures he loved to carve. I gather them all up, every feather, and they fill my hand. Resist the urge to run them along my cheekbone one last time. Breathe in the smell of his room instead, his little bed, the bookshelf full of comics. I wrap the feathery bunch in an old plastic bag, and Lewis takes it from me without a word as he goes off to do the evening feed.

Why did she do it? What would make anyone do such a thing? And a mother, too – how could she? I saw how she loved those children, how she worshipped Janosch, how she kissed little Katrina's head whenever she came close. Always together. When they were little I rarely saw her without the kids. But then lately, last year, before they stopped coming, she would often come alone, the kids no longer hanging from their mother's arm. Jan at the local school, doing well, she said. Loving science, biology, she said, pride creasing the lines around her eyes. Katrina, too shy, stayed home, did homework set by the council, helped her mother feed the chickens, mixed paint for her father.

She had looked tired, back then, and I had wondered if she was sick, if that was why she had kept her daughter home. Her straw-blonde hair hung limp around her angular face. Her eyes hollowed out, as if she had not slept in years. She missed home, she said. Missed the rain. I had laughed.

'The rain is different back home. It tastes of the mountains, of pine. And everything sings. You can hear the forest sing when it rains.'

I had topped up her cup of tea, given her another slice of lemon. I couldn't imagine what homesickness was like.

'I have another kind of homesickness,' I said, wanting to cheer her up. She had smiled. We had never talked about it before then. She knew about Cai, of course, but we had never talked of the elephant in the room – the fact I did not leave my house. I had not stepped over the threshold of my front door in over twenty-one years.

'But does it make you sick? Or would out there make you sick?' she said, scrutinising me with her blue eyes. I hadn't known what to say.

'It won't make me sick. I know that. I'm not scared, not really, or mad, despite what they might say about me in town! What have I got to be scared of now? I lost my boy. There is nothing the world out there can do to me that's worse.'

She nodded, stayed silent.

'I think I just prefer it in here. No surprises, you know? And he is everywhere in here.' Waved my hands around, vague.

She nodded again. She understood.

'Do you think the walls have eyes?' she asked. 'I think our house, your cottage, it watches me sometimes. As if it judging us, me. It has seen so much. And there we are, so small. These stones, they will outlast everything. It makes me feel a little... how do you say it... hopeless.' She had laughed, but it was a small laugh, small and sad.

'I think you may be right. But I'm not sure if they judge us. More like an audience who hasn't made up its mind who to support.'

She had fallen silent then, lost in thought.

I think back now and I wonder if I said the wrong thing. I can't remember if she came again after that visit. Maybe she did. Maybe I recollect it all wrong. But her words go round my head. Did she feel judged by us, by this landscape, by the old buildings? I could have done more. Homesickness. Indeed.

Her funeral came and went, and Lewis still hadn't been to see them. He promised he'd left them the feathers. The bag was gone the next morning, he said. It was a lovely service, apparently. No one wore black, which didn't surprise me. The family's wishes. Iwan said the children had been ever so reserved, thanked everyone, didn't cry. I imagine it, what it would have looked like, all those colourful clothes in the little village graveyard, the husband, with his long grey hair.

I never went to Cai's funeral. As if it would be possible to attend a thing like that. Lewis went, with his sister, of course, to help him through it. He never told me what it was like, and I didn't ask. The only detail I didn't want from the outside.

Iwan said the coroner came back with suicide, and the case was closed. He said there was ill health – she was very poorly. Dr Banner in town hinted there had been previous attempts. She could not be swayed. That in some ways the family was relieved, that she had suffered a long time, she had stopped making sense, talked of little else but how to end it. Though relieved is the wrong word, of course.

Lewis tells me one morning the husband came to see him, as he was checking on the cows. Said he wants to stay on. That his boy's back in school, his daughter staying home, 'For now.' I don't know if I am relieved or not.

The summer drags on. The cowshed stands empty, the cows gambolling with their calves in the high pasture. Lewis gets a tan, and the lines around his eyes deepen. He says I am losing weight, that I am too pale.

'I'm fine,' I tell him, 'no harm can come to me, in here.'

He says nothing, steps out into the glare of the afternoon, and I see to the dishes.

Then, on a hot still day, while Lewis is out slurrying, there is a knock at the door. Peering out of the kitchen window, I see them. They are holding hands, and whispering, as if sharing a great secret. The boy sees me, and smiles, waves, arm high up, as if I am far away.

'Hullo! We came to say thanks, for the gift.' Jan pauses, looks at his sister, unsure. Katrina has grown tall; she looks so like her mother it gives me pause as I take her in. Just as thin, but rangy, her hair a darker, muddier blonde. She does not meet my eye, but holds her brother's hand, a step behind him. I lean further out of the window, my mind racing. It has been so long.

'We came just to say thank you, but we saw... the tree...' Jan turns, and points behind him, out of my line of sight, to the end of the farmhouse. Katrina steps back, and points too.

'The fruit – there's so many. And they're ripe. We could make jam...' She trails off, as if scared of my response.

It takes me a moment to work out what they mean, then I realise. The damsons. They must be early – it's only the end of August, though it has been hot. I smile and nod. 'Of course! You're welcome – take them all,' I say.

Jan looks confused, then awkward, his big hands hanging by his side. 'We'll come back – we have no bags.'

'I'll get you a bag – please stay.' Before I can change my mind I pull my head inside, and go to get a bag from the kitchen. I get two – my best plastic carriers, the ones Lewis uses when he gets the shopping in the supermarket in town. Heading back to the window my feet suddenly change course, and I find I am walking towards my front door. Pulling up the latch, the bolt too. Drag back the heavy timbers, its base jamming against the slate tiles. And there they are, standing directly in front of me.

It only feels like yesterday they were sitting in my little kitchen and Jan was wandering around marvelling at Cai's collected treasures, Katrina too small to put down. They step back from me – out of fear, or politeness, I can't tell. Their eyes betray a sadness, a hollow cave I know too well. Many nights lying awake, with no answer even in the dawn, sunlit days that offend the heart. They are still in the early phase – there is so much more of it to come.

Suddenly some part of me wants to see the tree, the dusky impossible blue of the wild plums – to see if it is as full, the fruit as ripe as they say. I take a step, and then another, and my feet are on the sun-warmed stone flags in front of the house. They watch me, do not say a word. Jan holds out his hand to me, and Katrina smiles. I breathe in, and out, and take another step.

THE AIRING CUPBOARD

Sara Emmerton

Can words disappear? As if they've never been thought up? Like bubbles in the garden? Pop! Gone. Or else they're lost to the sky. Can people do that? Disappear? Be unthinked? Pop! Gone. Lost.

Edith's legs dangled from where she sat on the second shelf up, but there wasn't much room for dangling. Her nose touched the inside of the cupboard door and she smelt pine.

'You hot, too, Rufus?' Her cuddly mouse lay between her knees in the loose hammock of her school skirt. 'It's so stuffy in here. Stuffy. Stuffy. Stuf-fy.'

Edith's spit balls landed on Rufus's fur like snow on mud. Not that she could see much in the thick dark. She checked both sides of his pink felt ears, pulled through his white string tail. Nothing. Spider-wriggled her fingers deep into his soft body and kissed his tummy up and down. But she couldn't find her spit *or* her words. Not one of either.

Edith lifted Rufus close to her face. 'See?' She said to him, eyebrows lifted so high they snuck under the deep auburn curls of her fringe. Then she filled her cheeks with air and dragged her finger out of her left cheek. 'Pop! Gone. Lost.'

But the heat clogged up her chest. 'Hard to breathe in here, Rufus.'

Not enough air for speaking out loud, stupid. Not enough air or space. Think your words, stupid.

So Edith glued her lips shut and thought her words. She always did what Mr Kingsman said.

***

He set her the challenge on the evening of her ninth birthday.

Gin rummy. Her turn.

The kitchen door was closed. To dim the clattering and clinking of the clearing up, the radio turned loud over the running water and the finger-fluffing of bubbles. And the singing. Mum wanted to spare Mr Kingsman from *that*. What about Edith, though? She didn't want to be spared. She liked to know Mum was there, sweet and soft and happy and within reach. But nobody asked Edith. And the kitchen door was closed.

Edith sat on one end of the sofa with her legs tucked under her, skin squelchy against the conker-coloured leather, pins and needles in the tops of her feet and her toes. Mr Kingsman sat on the other end, stick legs reaching for the coffee table in the middle of the room, spindle-body twisted towards the cards and Edith.

Gin rummy. Her turn.

She checked the spray in her left hand. Jack and king and ace of diamonds. Just the queen for the run. She could win the game with a run like that.

Edith put two fingers on the card on the top of the pick-up pile, then slid her thumb under it.

Wait. Wish. Come on, queen. Be the queen. Red queen. Diamond queen.

And she was about to take it, to turn over the card. But just then Mr Kingsman leant towards her. Close in. Closer. The sofa breathed out behind him.

Reaching forwards, he covered her hand and her wrist with his hand. He rested it there. The back of his hand was like a mound of cracked pale earth. Her fingers trapped underneath.

Think of the hottest place in your house, Edith.

Diamond queen. Red queen. Diamond queen. Red queen. *The place you can make it work.*

Queen of diamonds. Queen of diamonds.

Reckon you can do it? Make things better, for once? Make things easier for everyone?

The oven. That was the hottest place in the house.

But the oven wouldn't work. Someone would find her. The door was dirty bronze with burnt pizza and old cooking smoke, but it was still see-through. Someone would hear the hum of the broken fan, come in to turn it off. Then there was the oven light. Hurt your eyes bright. White dazzle beams coming through the cracks at the bottom of the door. Giveaway.

Not the oven, then. Too many ways for her to be found.

Well? Mr Kingsman snatched back his hand, interlinking fingers from both of his hands, flipping them over and stretching his palms upwards, arms to the ceiling. Then he leant back on the sofa, his hands a nest for his head.

Without his palm, the back of Edith's hand was cold and bare. For a moment she felt naked, as if he'd snatched away every stitch of her summer dress. The cards stayed warm, though, and she laid her four fingers flat on the top of the pile.

Answer me!

Her answer?

The usual: Edith couldn't find her voice. Not even a whimper or a cough or a rumble-mutter sorry. And even if she had been able to speak to him, she wouldn't have known what to say. How to make things better. The usual: Edith, stupid and small. The usual: Edith, a waste of space and a waste of air.

The *un*usual: Edith knew just what to do. Edith knew just what she *would* do.

First, though. Wait. Wish. She turned over the top card. Jack of spades. That's decided it then, she thought.

* * *

It's not a game, Edith. Thought you'd know that by now.

It wasn't a game. Edith knew that by now. But the word filled her up anyway. G-A-M-E. Game. For the moment, it was the only word which existed. The only word which tumbled in and out of her. Her head pulsed with it. Game. Game. As if someone had pulled her hair into a bobble too hard. Game. Game. Forced the grips in at the back of her head. Game. Game. Game. When she was full, *game* spilled over into the dark airing cupboard. Like extra sheets, shoved in, any old how. Game. Or towels, folded. Game. Or socks, drying. The walls whispered it. Game. Game. Game. The shelves shouted it. Game. Game.

'Game,' Edith said. Rufus jumped, then fell between the slats.

No words, I said. No words. And for Christ's sake, no shouting in here.

Edith's freckles burned. Poppy face. Her school tights clung to the fronts of her knees, the backs of her thighs. Game. Game. Sweat slipped between her toes. Game. Game. Game.

116

She wanted it gone. Like the bubbles. Popped. Gone. Lost. She tried to pop it, she tried –

Game. Same. Game. Shame. Shame. Shame. Shame. Shame.

Edith's eyes stung at the inside corners. Not that word. Shame. Think of something else. Shame. Think of something else. Think of something else. Think of something else.

Something else: Rufus.

Edith reached down to grab the frayed ends of his tail. Her head pressed against the door and with a soft click the cupboard opened. A little light. A little air. Was that allowed?

What do you think, stupid?

She'd close it later. First, Edith squeezed her body flat and lifted herself back on to the second shelf. She put Rufus in her lap. She stroked his back, then turned him over and ruffled the old fur on his tummy. His poor tummy. His poorly tummy, which wouldn't get better. Not ever.

She pushed the fur from his marble eyes so that they were as big and as kind as Dad's eyes. Next, she tucked him under her chin, so he rested near her shoulder and she could smell him, she could almost taste him. Some of his grey wire whiskers scratched her neck, some of them tickled her jaw. His fur, old and rough, was like Dad's chin and cheeks before a shave.

Truth was, she couldn't look at Rufus without seeing Dad. Couldn't touch him without thinking her dad was there with her. Even here. Even now. She heard his trombone-boom voice making funny flute squeaks, piccolo squeaks sometimes. She heard Dad's stories over and over. Rufus eating through the bag of tinsel in the loft until there were gold and silver mouse pellets on the stairs. Rufus riding through the house on the hoover; then sliding down the bannisters. Wheeeee! Rufus sneaking into their holiday suitcase and learning to surf in Cornwall. Rufus, curled tight into a ball, crying, because the doctor had given him bad news about his tummy, his tummy that would never get better. Not ever.

Dad said you could tell the truth in stories. Dad said you could tell *your* truth in stories. She didn't understand the difference between the truth and *your* truth. But, but…

Truth was she missed Dad.

Mr Kingsman and Dad were Quaker friends. Mum didn't believe in all of that, and she didn't think that Edith should, either. Or at least Edith should make her own mind up about God and Quakers and Meeting Houses when she was older. So Edith stayed at home with Mum. But she still got to know Mr Kingsman, because he came for supper on Tuesdays, after the evening meeting.

First thing Mr Kingsman did, every week, was hang his suit jacket on the back of the chair. The pockets were spilling over with sweets. Lemon bonbons and orange barley sugars and brightly wrapped toffees. A chocolate éclair fell to the floor that first week. *Help yourself,* he mouthed to her. She did. She grabbed them from the floor and his pockets and his hands when he flashed the twists of the wrappers from closed fists behind his back.

They ate lasagne or macaroni cheese and blackcurrant cheesecake or strawberry cheesecake or chocolate cheesecake. They talked about grown-up things like local politics and music and European cities and schools and books.

'Call me Ray,' Mr Kingsman said. He asked her questions and nodded when she spoke. As if everything she said made sense. And mattered. As if she mattered.

Ray started to belong at their dinner table and in their family. On Tuesday nights.

When Dad died, Ray started to belong in their family on other nights. Every night. Then overnight.

He was Dad's friend. Dad had asked him to take care of Mum and Edith. That's what Ray said. Dad wanted this. Dad wanted Ray and Edith to be special friends. That's what he said.

Until he said: *Enough. Shameful little girl.* And that she should disappear. Make things better for everyone. Make things easier for everyone.

Shameful. ~~Shame.~~ Shame. Shame. Shame. ~~Shame.~~ Think of something else. ~~Shame.~~ Something else. Something else. Something else.

Something else, Rufus, was the airing cupboard. The airing cupboard was Vintage Cream. Like the wall. The spare tins said so. Vintage Cream (Landing and Airing Cupboard). They'd even painted the metal hinges in the same colour, so the cupboard sank into the wall and when you looked up from the porch there was a gold jewel stuck on the wall with no reason and no purpose.

But the jewel had a reason and a purpose, didn't it? It opened a place to...

A place to...

Game. ~~Game.~~ Same. Shame. Shame. Shame.

A place to...

Hide.

Nobody looked for you in the airing cupboard. Not properly. Not for longer than it took to click the jewel door open then shut again. They'd see the sheets and the spare blankets on the pine shelves. They'd breathe in the warm thick dark. 'Nope, not there,' they'd mutter to themselves. 'No space for a person in there.'

They were wrong. There was space for a person. There was space for Edith.

The space for Edith to do it, to make things better, make things easier for everyone, was at the bottom of the cupboard. There was a square tile of old carpet on the cupboard floor. Like the mats they put in cars for your feet. Hard and scratchy.

Mum kept the towels here, folding them in half and stacking them into multi-coloured towers. Whole rainbows of bright colours. Before Edith started school, they used to sit on the landing and build the towers together. Higher and taller until the piles leaned like Pisa and fell like the Empire. Edith didn't know what Mum meant by Pisa or Empire, but she laughed because Mum laughed and they laughed into their arms and their feet and their toes.

But when Edith looked down at the towels now that she was nine, they were grey.

Stop the words. It's nearly time.

The door was still ajar. Edith breathed in a massive breath of the landing air, then squeezed herself down from the slats. Pushed the towel towers over and crawled into her space behind them. Here, she hunched herself over like a woodlouse. Or maybe a tortoise, its wrinkled head tucked inside its shell. She put Rufus on the floor in front of her head.

Tortoise. She liked that word. How had she not noticed it before? The way you stretch your mouth out long like a trumpet then bring it up in a smile, like you have to smile for it, you absolutely have to?

Stop the words. Time now, Edith.

She reached her right arm forwards. Her fingernails scraped the pine edging of the door. And she pulled it, she pulled it...

Shut. Click. Done.

Dark.

A different dark to before. Stern. The breath inside her stuck like bread clumped at the back of her mouth. Or was it the top of her throat? What did it matter? Words didn't matter any more, did they? Not mouth or stern or throat or dark or breath or bread. Not tortoise, said with a smile. Not game or shame or popped or gone or lost.

Edith: Popped. Gone. Lost.

Stop the fucking words.

Air didn't last for ever, did it? That was why you had to let the spider out. It would use up the air in the jar and it wouldn't be able to breathe and then and then—

I said, stop the fucking words.

Less air. Less air. Nearly gone. Nearly used up. Less air. Less air. Less air.

Edith gulped. Is that what the spider did, under the jar? Sucked up as much as it could, as fast as it could? She gulped. She gulped.

Her head hurt. A hundred screams all at once. She covered her eyes with her fingers. Hot tears ran on to the insides and outsides of her hands. Wouldn't stop. Wouldn't stop. Her tears dropped on to Rufus. On to the carpet. On to Rufus. On to Rufus. More tears. She buried her nose deep into Rufus's fur. Turned her head and rested her cheek on his back.

And then...

Her nose, damp. Her cheek, damp. Not hot damp like the tears that wouldn't stop. Cold damp from wet mouse fur. She snatched at her breath. 'Rufus!'

His fur was soaked with her tears. He was full of them. He was full of her dad. Her dad's stories. Her dad's words. She'd found them. Not popped. Not lost. Not gone.

'Not this, Edie.' Edith searched Rufus's wet drooped ears. 'I don't want this for you.'

But Dad's voice was weak and quiet. Like it had been in the hospital. His words thin and grey and too late it was too late.

She couldn't breathe. No more air. No more air. Too hot. Too weak. She couldn't breathe. No more air. No more air. Too hot. Too weak. Too hot. Too weak. No more air. No more air.

But then…

The trombone notes came, low and deep and strong. 'Not any of this.' From the pine walls and the slats of the shelves. 'Not Ray. Not this. Not any of this.' From the towel towers. From Rufus's wet fur. From herself. From herself. 'Tell someone, Edie love. Tell someone.'

Edith needed air. Edith wanted air. She wanted to breathe. She wanted to live.

With the ends of her strength, she pushed the towels aside and leant on the inside of the door.

Click. Open. Light. Light.
Air. Air. Air. Air.

Towels spilled out after her. Whole rainbows of them. Bright rainbows.

Rufus tumbled out next. Edith grabbed him. Held him to her face. Kissed his poorly tummy. More tears came. They mixed with the cool air. They mixed with her life.

'Mum!' Edith called, stumbling through the tingles of her feet and her legs until she stood tall and strong. 'Mum! Mum!'

She would tell her story.

She would tell the truth.

She would tell *her* truth.

ABOUT THE WRITERS

Helen O Neill was a GP in Ireland for nearly thirty years before retiring to become full-time carer to her wife. The change of pace allowed time to write, something she had always enjoyed doing but could rarely find time for. During the pandemic she took a Creative Writing course in Maynooth University. She was shortlisted for the RTÉ Francis McManus Short Story Competition in 2021, and also has prizes for flash fiction and poetry. She is a regular contributor on RTÉ radio's *Word In Edgeways*. In 2023 she took first place in the Curae Prize for non-fiction. She lives with her wife in Dublin.

Jessica Moxham is a writer from London. Her work is mostly focused on parenting, disability and how our attitudes towards these things shift. Jessica's memoir, *The Cracks that Let the Light In*, was published in 2021 and is about everything she learned during the first decade of raising her eldest, disabled son. She is currently studying for a Master's in Creative and Life Writing at Goldsmiths, working on fiction and non-fiction. Jessica trained as an architect and lives with her husband and three children in the house that she designed to suit her family.

Sheena Hussain is a British Pakistani poet, writer and essayist; a non-practising immigration lawyer who turned to poetry after receiving a cancer diagnosis. 'No Thanks', a piece of creative non-fiction, was shortlisted for the inaugural Curae Prize in 2023. 'Watching a Green Fly' was longlisted for the Leeds Poetry Festival Competition 2022. She is widely anthologised and is the founder of Poem:99, an international children's poetry competition. She is a member of Inscribe – Peepal Tree Press's writer's development programme. When she is not writing, you will find her hiking in mountains and taking long solitary walks.

Kerry Mead writes creative non-fiction and fiction and studied Creative and Critical Writing at Birkbeck College, University of London. She is passionate about writing about neurodivergence, place and everything that makes us human. Her work has been published in *The Mechanics Institute Review* and *Oranges Journal*. Away from the world of literary writing Kerry is a music writer and reviewer, and was previously Chief Culture Editor for *The Everyday Magazine*. She lives in Bristol with her two children, a haughty cat, a grumpy tortoise and eighty-three houseplants.

Joyanna Lovelock is a Barrister-at-Law. An academic lawyer, she has worked as a law lecturer, legal trainer and examiner. She was appointed to the magisterial bench in 1991 and she was a candidate for the Professional Doctorate in Criminal Justice at Portsmouth University Institute of Criminal Justice Studies. Her non-fiction has appeared in *The Lawyer*, *The Gleaner UK* and *The Voice*. She has also spent some time pro-ducing and publishing her own general-interest magazine in

London, and she has been a newspaper columnist, where she shared her musings and observations on modern life and the big issues of the day seasoned with her signature humour and wit. Her columns were published in book form in 2019 under the title *Let Me Tell You Something*, which went on to be a finalist in two international book awards (2020 and 2021). She currently shares her musings and observations on her blog (www.letmetellyou.co.uk), which has recently won a major global award as well as being longlisted for Yeovil's 'Writing Without Restrictions' prize. Two years ago she created a crime podcast (www.btytpodcast.com), in which she researches and narrates a murder case from time past – usually those with a controversial outcome – and she also interviews individuals who have had a lived experience with the Criminal Justice System. As well as being the host, she is also the producer, and these efforts have been rewarded in a global gold award in 2023.

Kate Blincoe is a nature writer and contributor to the *Guardian*'s Country Diary. Passionate about wildlife and sustainability, when she's not writing about the environment she is often found knee-deep in a stream or striding through woodland. She is the author of *The No-Nonsense Guide to Green Parenting*, and is currently working on fiction projects.

Emma Gow is a Scottish writer who lives on the south-east coast of Scotland with her husband, three children and dog. She studied English Literature and Philosophy at the University of Glasgow, and was shortlisted for the Penguin Christmas Love Story Competition in 2021. When she isn't at work or trying to finish editing her work in progress, she can most likely be found watching a Kdrama or reading something from the never-ending pile of books at the end of her bed. She is delighted to be included in the Curae anthology, and is most grateful to Anna Vaught, the judges, Renard Press and all the supporters of the prize.

Jan Kaneen is a mum, sister, wife, daughter, auntie, grandparent, carer and, now, writer. She was born and bred in Bolton, Lancashire, but lives, these days, below sea level in the flat washes of the Cambridgeshire Fens, where she worries about the climate crisis whilst writing sometimes prize-winning stories about dangerous places. She has an MA in Creative Writing (with distinction) from the Open University and has, most recently, won the Bath novella-in-flash competition with her story *A Learning Curve*, which is available from Ad Hoc Fiction. Her short story collection, *Hostile Environments*, is forthcoming from Northodox Press.

Feline (pronounced *Falina* – she's named after the little deer friend Bambi makes in the original German book by Felix Salten) was born in Germany, but grew up in the wilds of north Wales. She was home-schooled to the age of ten, learning about mosses and birds and listening to plays on the radio. She has lived in Berlin, northern France, Cornwall and London. Feline has had many jobs, from river surveyor to pizza chef, but recent chronic illness and needing to care for her youngest son, who has Cystic Fibrosis, means she is turning to her writing more than ever before. She has three children, and recently moved to south Devon. She has a number of fiction and non-fiction pieces due out in print this year, including an essay in the *Moving Mountains* anthology, published by Footnote Press and edited by Louise Kenward. Feline is currently working on the edits of a novel.

Sara Emmerton has always written stories. From first chapters under her duvet by torchlight when she was six, to her fourth full manuscript some forty years later, she hasn't stopped. Not during her degree (History of English Language, First Class), or postgraduate diploma in speech therapy before working on hospital wards with patients who had suffered strokes. Not when she dipped more than her toe into sea swimming off the Kent coast, or when she started a family of children – not to mention cats. All along, she has strived to develop her skills, learning from author-mentors such as Anstey Harris, Stella Duffy and Heidi James, and she was delighted to be longlisted in 2022 for the Bridge Awards Emerging Writer award at Moniack Mhor. Parenting an autistic child turned Sara into a full-time carer in 2008, threatening to sap every last kilojoule of her energy. But little did she know, her caring role would give her even more reason and creative urge to tell her stories...

About Anna Vaught:
Anna Vaught is an English teacher, mentor and author of several books, including *Saving Lucia* (published to national acclaim in Italy as *Bang Bang Mussolini*), *Famished*, *Ravished*, *These Envoys of Beauty*, *The Zebra and Lord Jones* and *The Alchemy*. 2023 also sees the publication of the *Curae* anthology of short prose from the winning entrants to the prize she established in 2023 for writer-carers; and in 2024 her first essay collection, *To Melt the Stars*, is due to be

published. Her shorter and multi-genre works are widely published in journals, magazines and anthologies. Until recently, she was a columnist for *Mslexia*, and has written regularly for *The Bookseller*, including as a columnist. With a background in secondary English, mentoring with young people and community arts, Anna is now a guest university lecturer, tutor for Jericho Writers and teaches occasionally at secondary level. She works alongside chronic illness, and is a passionate campaigner for mental health provision and SEND support for young people. She is the mother of three sons, comes from a large Welsh family and lives in Wiltshire. She is a PhD candidate at York St John from December 2023–24, undertaking a PhD by Published Works on Magical Realism and Trauma, foregrounding her own work.

ACKNOWLEDGEMENTS

I must begin by saying that I worry I will have forgotten someone, because the deluge of help was extraordinary. So, in no particular order, love, thanks and respect from me – from us – to the following for making this happen. *It is quite a list.*

Lorraine Rogerson – thank you for the generous bursaries to our winners. I am grateful to the Arvon Foundation for their offer of online workshops, to clinical psychologist and writer Stephanie Carty for the places on her Psychology of Character course with a one-to-one Zoom follow-up, to Hannah Weatherill, Head of Media Rights at Penguin Random House for the workshop and showcase for all our shortlisted and winning writers, writer, Sarah Hilary for mentoring specifically for a carer who is also chronically ill or disabled, and to Sarah Rigby, director of leading independent publisher Elliot and Thompson for book coaching. Thank you *Mslexia* magazine for a subscription and a copy of the latest edition of your invaluable Guide to Indie Presses plus ta specifically to editor Debbie Taylor for featuring Curae in the winter edition. Thank you, author Claire Allan, for mentoring support, Jenny Savill, Managing Director of

Andrew Nurnberg Ltd Literary Agency, for one-to-one agent mentoring, and the same to Clare Coombes at the Liverpool Literary Agency, and to the Good Literary Agency for their kind support. Kit de Waal came forward to mentor – hooray – and Aaron Kent, author and publisher, came in at short notice to offer some dedicated poetry mentoring. Enormous appreciation for author and teacher Michael Langan for offering mentoring for an LGTBQIA+ author and to author Amy Lord for additional mentoring for a shortlisted writer. Editor and Cheshire Prize creator Sara Naidine Cox has been beside me all the way, giving advice and support. All the authors you see in the book have had the benefit of the Cheshire Prize summer school and its extended provision. Thanks to the *Bookseller* for profiling the book – and me! Also, it is great that our union, the Society of Authors, got behind this from the beginning, publishing me on their blog, offering free union memberships to our two winners and allowing me to showcase the prize at the 2023 AGM. Author Jennie Godfrey mentored an individual identifying as a working-class author and offered a place on a course from the Curtis Brown Creative portfolio. You are a star. Thank you for a beautiful curated reading list for each winner by bookworm and leading book blogger Clare 'Years of Reading Selfishly' Reynolds, and for helping profile the book and its authors and the cause behind it in publication week; props to Melissa Addey for offering the two winners a place on her excellent self-publishing workshop at the British Library and a raft of resources, and to Jericho Writers for the resources they gave and their interest in the book, to writer Jilly Whitehouse for a very generous book token for our two overall winners and to Aki Schilz at The Literary Consultancy for advice and ideas.

ACKNOWLEDGEMENTS

Thank you thank you to THE WONDERFUL Curae judges Michael Langan, Elissa Soave and Amy Lord. Between them there is a wealth of writing – fiction, editing and non-fiction – and teaching, and I will always be grateful for the cheerful, loving and diligent way they worked with me to read the many entries and discuss them all carefully. We all know what it is to be lifted up by others, and I shall talk more about that as we are underway, because all three were immensely supportive to me in my own challenges as we worked together on the prize. Finally, to Will at Renard Press for all he has done to make this book happen, including giving his time for free. Beyond this, I must thank him for the kindness and support he has shown me – not just for this book. He is a diamond in the publishing world, and I make no apologies for causing the inevitable embarrassment here.

Finally, thank you to all the people whose work you see in this book, to our honourable mentions Elaine Gregerson, Philip Forsyth, Poppy O'Neill and A.V. Bruce, and to ALL the many people who entered this inaugural Curae Prize. Many entrants wrote to me to tell me about their circumstances and what they were managing, the joys as well as the sad, very difficult things. We also had bereavements while the judging process was ongoing. At home I gave over a little corner of the garden, and with the entrants' permission planted a climbing rose for their lost loved ones. It is my profound hope that the Prize, its book and the communities which have formed around it can comfort and encourage us all.

RESOURCES AND IDEAS

The two charities to whom all profits are donated are the Carers' Trust (carers.org) and Carers UK (carersuk.org).

Here you will find a raft of information about support, advice on finance, health and how you can look after yourself. I would like to draw attention to the report recently published by the latter, the *State of Caring 2023*, which found that 27% of all unpaid carers had bad or very bad mental health. Caring may well come with financial hardship, and here will be advice. They can also advise you how to apply for **carers' allowance** – it is not a lot, and I have a great deal to say on that topic – and in addition, a **needs assessment** for the cared-for person. I would always speak to your **local carers' group or association**, or perhaps your **local council** (or the above charities), to find out what resources there are in your area and to request what is called a Carers' Assessment, as there may be things that can be locally funded in order to give you a break; counselling is offered in some areas. It is a good idea to make your GP aware of your role, and to ask at your local health centre about any relevant local groups. You will also find that some of the charities have online meet-ups and, if there is a local carers' group, a great deal may happen, to include helpful signposting for specific care needs – the things dependent on your role, such as provision for the child or young person in your care. In terms of having a break of any kind, there is information on this on the two websites above, but there is a brilliant charity in its infancy which we recommend: this is **Carefree** (carefreespace. org/take-a-break), which offers full-time (that is, over thirty hours a week) carers one or two nights away in a hotel, B&B or holiday cottage, year-round, once a year. Breakfast is generally included, and in addition to travel there is a £25 administration fee payable.

One thing we know: you cannot pour from an empty cup. Carers get very, very tired. As I say elsewhere, the role is predicated on love, but please do all you can – even if it is tiny increments – to look after you. We all hope that the Curae project, the book and the funds it will raise are also an encouragement. I would like to end with comments from some of our wonderful Curae Prize writers. It will not only be me who is crying in a moment. Thank you to all of you, and I am so glad you have found one another.

ANNA VAUGHT
November 2023

COMMENTS FROM
THE WRITERS

Helen

Writing while caring is an art in itself, trying to find snatches of time then getting into the zone without preamble. Most of my writing as a result is short work. When I won the Curae prize, I felt seen as a carer for the first time.

Jessica

Curae is the first prize I have seen that seemed designed for me. I had been working on a non-fiction piece and the push to get it ready for Curae was the jolt I needed. I am trying to balance the responsibilities of caring for my son with the desire to write about the realities of our lives together, which is a practical and intellectual challenge. The Curae Prize not only makes space for carers like me to put forward, and value, their writing, but also creates a sense of solidarity.

Sheena

A platform I had been searching for some time finally found me. I knew entering would mean empathy and compassion. Although writing about the caring side was not essential,

I decided to write about it anyway. It's a candid account of the realities of caring for my mama. I wrote it nearly in one sitting on my respite day.

Kerry

I started writing in 2016 when I became a registered carer for my oldest child. Creative writing started as a space to wind down and be myself, not just 'Mum', which I could access in quiet moments without having to arrange childcare or even leave the house. As I wrote more and realised I was good at it, writing became more than a hobby or creative outlet, but something I felt deeply passionate about.

Finding time to write is hard when you are a parent; it is even harder when your child has additional needs, when all the time spent advocating, on life admin and the late nights and early mornings can feel like a demanding full-time job. The writing industry is incredibly crowded and competitive, and caring can be emotionally exhausting as well as taking up much of your time, so I have often wondered if I have not just enough time, but also the energy needed to try and make it as a writer. I stumbled across a Twitter (X) post about the Curae Prize in late 2022. Even though I had not entered any writing prizes before, I knew I had to submit something to this one. It was exciting to see all the well-known names in the publishing industry who had offered up their time or prizes, who obviously felt passionate about helping to give a voice to carers when we can often feel invisible and overlooked by society.

Making the shortlist was a big shock. Winning a place on a writing course, ongoing support from Anna and a session with an agent has been fantastic, but more importantly, we winners and shortlistees have since formed our own small community of writers – cheering each other on from the sidelines and sharing our lives and experiences as carers who also happen to be writers. Everyone who is a carer or writer knows how important it is for your well-being to have a support network, but becoming part of a community of writers who understand the pressures of caring is priceless. It has given me that energy I need to keep on going and keep on writing, and it is something I am sure I would never have come across without the Curae.

Joyanna
To be shortlisted gave me unspeakable joy. Being shortlisted for such a prestigious prize is an uplifting and incredible gift.

Kate
As a carer, your needs so often come last on the list, and you can sometimes feel like you have lost yourself. Curae has brought me such a boost of confidence that me and my words matter. The prize comes with amazing opportunities to learn, with courses and contacts, as well as a beautiful group of the other shortlisted writer-carers, giving us a place to share resources and inspiration with other people who understand. It has reminded me not to look inward, or at what I cannot do amongst the stress or restrictions, but to always strive for what is still possible. And writing fits into a life of caring better than most things! When home feels like a prison, you can write your way out between the bars. When you have swallowed down your voice again, to do the right thing, you can still cast off your silence on the page. When you are busy with the ongoing mundane, you can travel and

create and fly in your head, just waiting, just itching for the time to write. It is a quiet little miracle that saves us.

Emma Gow

Being part of the Curae Prize has been invaluable and hugely life-enriching for me. A lot of my time is taken up advocating for and tending to the needs of those I care for and I struggle at times to make my own voice heard, and writing is one of my few creative outlets. To have my writing seen and valued like this has been immeasurably confidence-boosting and given me the push to keep going. I am so fortunate to have been included in such a warm, supportive and inspiring group of fellow writers, and I am looking forward to reading and sharing in everyone's successes in the future.

Jan

I entered Curae at an all-time low, co-caring for two elderly relatives, one who had had a stroke in the second lockdown and was deteriorating fast and stuck, bedbound in a downstairs open-plan space shared with her housebound husband who also had complex medical needs. Desperate to inject some positivity into my carer's journey I made myself write, edit and send my story into the comp, and when it was shortlisted, I wept. I have been shortlisted a lot and am not prone to weeping, but these were carer's tears that so needed crying. But more than that, in bringing the shortlistees together, Curae has given me, *us*, a like-minded community of writer-carers who understand the challenges of navigating the denuded waters of health and social care whilst trying to put words down, and that is the best writing prize I have ever won. True story. Not the end.

Feline

The Curae Prize is a recognition of the enormous challenges we as writer-carers quietly overcome to express ourselves creatively. It has meant finding community and confidence, and most importantly, it is a platform from which to celebrate those voices society might not otherwise hear from. I am a parent-carer, as well as having my own chronic illness. Entering and then being shortlisted for the Curae was the kick I needed to take my writing, and myself as a writer, seriously. I now call myself a writer – something I did not dare do before.

Sara

Change one letter and the Curae Prize becomes the Curae Pride, and pride is what the prize has meant to me. In entering and being shortlisted, I have seen myself for the first time as a writer-carer and not 'just a writer' or 'just a carer'. I am proud of how the two roles complement and contribute to each other, compassion and creativity being key in both. I am proud of trying my best in both. And thanks to the Curae Prize, for once – because often there is just not the time, the space or the energy – I am simply proud of myself.

The Curae Prize will run again in 2025.
https://thecuraeprize.uk